CATERPILLARS
AND THEIR MOTHS

CATERPILLARS
AND THEIR MOTHS

BY

IDA MITCHELL ELIOT
AND
CAROLINE GRAY SOULE

WITH ILLUSTRATIONS FROM PHOTOGRAPHS
OF LIVING CATERPILLARS AND SPREAD MOTHS
BY EDITH ELIOT

NEW YORK
THE CENTURY CO.
1921

WE DEDICATE THIS BOOK TO THE
TEACHERS AND CHILDREN WHO
HAVE BEGGED US TO WRITE IT

PREFACE

AFTER more than twenty years of studying and rearing moths, of much hunting for information which was not always to be found, of answering the many questions of many children, parents, and teachers, we have decided to put the results of a part of our experience into a form which may help beginners to avoid our mistakes, to escape the ill results of ignorance, and to get more satisfaction with less failure than we had. Therefore we have tried to put into this book all the facts needed for successful work in rearing moths, as much structural detail as beginners need to know, an account of the appliances we have found most useful, and a list of the books which we have used most.

To this information we have added life-histories of forty-three species which may be found throughout a wide range of our country, and of each species we have given a picture of the larva and the moth, male and female being shown when they differ much. These life-histories are not taken from the accounts of other persons, but are exact statements of our own experiences and experiments. They are not given as general statements, because we have learned that the experience with one brood of caterpillars may be quite dif-

ferent from that with another brood of the same
species, and that even individuals of the same brood,
reared under the same conditions, may vary in size,
coloring, marks, habits, and length of the larval stage
of life, and therefore general statements about one
might not be true of another.

It is the tendency to generalize from a small experience which makes many of the popular books on this
subject, as on other branches of nature work, un-
trustworthy and thus of little value.

For details of structure and function we have supplemented our own knowledge by consulting Dr.
Packard's "Text-book of Entomology," a book to
which we owe much.

The names of the moths are those given in Dr. John
B. Smith's "List of Lepidoptera of Boreal America,"
which is standard now, and their meanings are given
when they could be found. All names do not have
meanings. For instance, there is no appropriateness in
cecropia, *hylæus*, *astylus*, and many others. Some names
are made up from Greek or Latin roots and termina-
tions, and some moths are simply "named for" entomologists, historical or mythological characters, or
called by Indian names. One English entomologist is
credited with mixing a lot of letters in a hat, drawing
out a certain number, and then combining them to
form names, *Datana*, *Nadata*, and *Tanada* being some
of the names so formed. The nomenclature of moths
may be considered purely arbitrary. We have accented
the syllables according to the best authorities.

We have not attempted to give full details of internal
structure or function, but only such as affect the rear-

ing of larvæ or the treatment of eggs, pupæ, or moths.
Further details may be found in Packard's "Text-
book of Entomology."

We owe thanks to Miss Edith Eliot for her unfailing
patience in photographing our caterpillars, which need
more patience than any other " sitters " except, perhaps,
birds; to Dr. A. S. Packard for the meanings of many
names; to Dr. A. G. Mayer for reading the structural
part for us; to Mr. D. W. Coquillett and Dr. William H.
Ashmead for lists of the parasitic flies preying upon
caterpillars; to the children who have brought us
specimens; and to Mr. M. V. Slingerland for the use
of his excellent photograph of *Dryocampa rubicunda*
larvæ, larvæ which we could not get when we wished
to photograph them.

We have written a true book, and we hope that it
may prove a helpful one. If it is not interesting, the
fault is with us, not with the subject.

CONTENTS

PART I

THE CRAWLERY

CONTENTS

PART I

THE CRAWLERY

APPLIANCES, METHODS OF WORK,
STRUCTURE OF MOTHS, ETC.

CATERPILLARS AND THEIR MOTHS

I

THE CRAWLERY

WE were sitting in a room which had recently been added to the house, and for which the whole family had been suggesting names appropriate to our work on insects—or supposed to be. So far none had suited us, and we were busy, in a nameless room, cleaning out our caterpillar-tins and putting into them fresh leaves for the caterpillars. A sister of One of Us stood at the door watching us, and suddenly exclaimed: "Ugh! I don't see how you can do it! It makes me crawl all over just to see them."

"Thank you!" cried the Other of Us. "Our room has its name! Since most of its occupants are crawlers and some of its visitors 'crawl,' it shall be the Crawlery!"

It has been the Crawlery for so many years now that some of the sister's children, although well grown up, cannot remember it as anything else.

The Crawlery is full of associations. It has witnessed

3

the birth of many a rare caterpillar and its career to the "perfect insect" or to an untimely and much-lamented death. It has witnessed our struggles, in the beginning of our work, for a knowledge which no book gave us, our experiments in ways of caring for our crawlers, our discoveries with regard to their structure and habits, our successes and our failures. It has heard — if "walls have ears" — our desperate declarations that when we wrote a book about moths and caterpillars it should contain every detail of which we had felt the need and which we had had to learn by years of observation, experiment, study, and repeated failure.

The Crawlery is a most convenient and pleasant room, with a north window for our microscope and a west window in front of which is a wide shelf, used as a table when we work over our caterpillars and holding our scissors, forceps, magnifiers, and cleaning-brushes, with an empty tin or two.

Opposite are our book-shelves, which hold our working library:

> Gray's "Manual of Botany,"
> Britton and Brown's "Illustrated Flora,"
> Wood's "Class Book of Botany,"
> Newton's "Dictionary of Birds,"
> Chapman's "Hand-book of Birds,"
> Coues' "Key to North American Birds,"
> Packard's "Text-book of Entomology,"
> Packard's "Monograph on the Bombycine Moths,"
> Packard's "Guide to the Study of Insects,"
> Packard's "Forest Insects,"
> Scudder's "Butterflies,"

Scudder's " Every-day Butterflies,"
Smith's " List of Lepidoptera of Boreal America,"
Smith's " Sphingidæ,"
Beutenmüller's " Descriptive Catalogue of Sphingidæ
Found within Fifty Miles of New York,"
Beutenmüller's " Descriptive Catalogue of Bombycidæ
Found within Fifty Miles of New York,"
Edwards' " Bibliographical Catalogue of the Described
Transformations of Lepidopterous Insects,"
Comstock's " Manual for the Study of Insects,"
Fernald's " Sphingidæ,"
Harris' " Insects Injurious to Vegetation,"
Saunders' " Insects Injurious to Fruits,"
Grote's " Sphingidæ,"
French's " Butterflies of the Eastern United States,"
Dyar's " Classification of Lepidopterous Larvæ,"
Fernald's " Orthoptera of New England,"
Emerton's " Spiders,"
Hentz's " Spiders,"
The various Reports and Bulletins of the United States
Department of Agriculture, of the Agricultural De-
partments of several of the States, and of Experiment
Stations; the Proceedings, Transactions, and other
publications of various Entomological Societies; " Au-
thor's Extras," bound volumes of " Psyche," " The
Canadian Entomologist," " Entomological News," and
other magazines.

On the lowest shelf are our note-books and the larger
books containing the daily records of the lives of lepidopterous insects which we have reared from egg to
imago.

In the closet there are boxes of photographic nega-
tives of our caterpillars and moths; writing-materials;

bottles of chloroform, alcohol, naphtha, ink, and glue;
boxes of rubber bands, gummed labels, insect-pins,
chopped sphagnum, and pieces of scrim cut to fit the
different boxes; setting-boards; pipettes for applying
naphtha or chloroform to doomed insects; and wooden
boxes, pasteboard boxes, and empty larva-tins of all
sizes and shapes, from the smallest round pill-boxes to
large, square-cornered citron-boxes, all with covers
which shut over their edges. The closet drawers hold
balls of twine, rolls of wrapping-paper, blotting-paper,
old cotton, and large pieces of netting, lace, and scrim.

The room has shelves around the walls, and on these
shelves stand the caterpillar-tins and insect-cages in
use, while on the lower shelf, close by the door, are
tumblers to put over moths and tin boxes to hold
caterpillars brought by the children, to whose kindness
we owe many a fine specimen. On a low set of
drawers for spread specimens stands our large butterfly cage. Under the shelves are large tin boxes for the
food-plants of the caterpillars, and our tin collecting-
boxes, a large pail of water for freshening the twigs
collected for food, and a large waste-basket.

The Crawlery is our best working-place, because
here we have every convenience, but we have done
much "crawling" in other rooms and with scant
supplies of everything but tin boxes, scrim, rubber
bands, caterpillars, and patience. The Crawlery is not
a necessity, but it is a great help and satisfaction.

Our out of doors equipment is very simple, consist-
ing of small pocket tins for eggs and small caterpillars,
tin pails or larger tin boxes for larger larvæ, our
"botany-box" or "vasculum" for the leaves we must

get to feed our voracious caterpillars, a net, and an umbrella with a rectangular "crook" at the end of the handle. The umbrella serves as a long arm to pull down boughs just out of reach. For boughs still more out of reach One of Us carries in her pocket a length of strong fish-line with a sinker on one end. By throwing this well over the bough the sinker will carry the line down on the other side, and the branch can be pulled down very easily.

Sharp eyes, patience, and accuracy are absolutely essential to our work in the Crawlery and out of doors.

II

EGGS AND CATERPILLARS

WHEN we began studying moths and caterpillars we knew that these caterpillars hatched from eggs, ate for a time, then became pupæ,— either in cocoons or out of them,— and finally emerged as moths which mated and laid eggs for another brood. The eggs were the last form which we found, but we shall begin our account of the structure and development of the moth with the egg because it is the first stage of the individual.

Most of our sphingid moths, often called hawk-moths, lay small, green, ovoid or globular eggs, and place them singly on a leaf, twig, tendril, or among flower-buds. These eggs usually become yellow or yellow-white before hatching, and have shells so transparent that the larvæ may be seen, curled up in them, for a day or two before they eat their way out.

Most of our large satur'niids lay opaque white eggs, often stained with the brown gummy substance which fastens them to the leaf or twig, and these eggs usually turn lead-colored before hatching. Some of these moths lay their eggs in a row of two or more close together, or in two or more rows. Sometimes there are so many rows that they make a mat, as we have

8

seen *cynthia* lay them, and occasionally other rows are laid on top of the first mat, as *cynthia* lays them sometimes but not always. Eggs laid singly are found once in a while, but not often.

Most of our ceratocam'pids lay yellow eggs like drops of honey or amber, and place them singly or in groups on leaves or twigs. These eggs become redder or browner before hatching, and are transparent enough to show the larvæ for the last day or two.

Moth eggs vary in form, some being ovoid, others like cream-peppermints, some cylindrical, others globular or hemispherical, and others shaped more like wafers than anything else. Some eggs are smooth, some ridged, and some have the surface marked like hammered silver. Some, like those of *Attacus angulifera*, are smooth except at one end, which looks like hammered silver or honeycomb. The shell is brittle and stiff with chitin, and breaks easily. At one end, usually, is the micropyle. This may be one opening or canal leading into the egg, or it may be a group of such canals. Through one of these openings the spermatozoön enters the egg and fuses with the egg-nucleus, fertilizing the egg and giving rise to the new caterpillar.

The length of the egg-period varies from five days to four weeks, except in the case of such eggs as are laid in the summer or autumn and hatch in the following spring or summer.

When their time comes the little caterpillars nibble holes in their shells and crawl out, looking altogether too large to have lain curled up in the egg-shell. As soon as they are out of the shell the different kinds

show different habits.   Some stay in one place for a
long time, as if resting or growing strong; others crawl
about as fast as they can; some turn around and
rapidly devour the shells from which they have just
come; others eat a part of the shell and eat it slowly;
others take much rapid exercise before eating any of
the shell; and still others crawl as far away from their
shells as they can before feeding or resting.   It may
be nearly a day before the young caterpillars begin to
eat the leaves; indeed, the tent-caterpillars often hatch
before there are any leaves to eat and have to wait for
them to open.   All the caterpillars we have reared
have been eager for water and have drunk thirstily the
drops sprinkled on the leaves.

A caterpillar is made up of a head with its appendages, and a body divided into rings or segments, with
their appendages.   The thoracic segments of the body
are the first three behind the head.   The other segments are the abdominal segments.   In our descriptions of caterpillars the " first segment " is that next
the head.

The head is made up of a few segments so closely
held together that they seem one piece with lines, or
sutures, showing the divisions.   The eyes are the sim-
plest form of eyes, *ocel'li*, and can distinguish only light
and darkness, so that caterpillars cannot be said to see
at all.   The mouth-parts are placed at the lower part
of the head and may be watched in action very easily.

The mouth-parts of a caterpillar are the *la'brum*, or
" upper lip," the mandibles or true cutting jaws with
which the caterpillar bites off bits of the leaf; the first
pair of *maxil'læ*, which bite the piece smaller and help

hold it; and the second pair of maxillæ, which make the "under lip" and are joined in one piece. The first maxillæ carry the *pal'pi*, or feelers.

When the caterpillar comes from the egg its head is very large in proportion to its body, but the size of the head does not change until the larva molts, while the body grows so much that often the head looks small in proportion before molting-time comes. The head is stiff with chitin, and when the caterpillar molts, the old head-covering, which is called a mask, is pushed off in one piece, usually transparent, color-less, and hard as the transparent celluloid which it resembles. Caterpillars' heads are flat, or nearly so, across the front, wider and longer than they are thick, and vary in shape from almost round to the shape of an apple-seed with the pointed end uppermost.

Among the mouth-parts of the caterpillar opens a little tube called the spinneret. This tube is the outer end of a duct which connects with the silk-glands in the abdomen. When the caterpillar wishes to spin, it forces the gummy fluid secreted by these glands to the mouth of the spinneret, applies it first to some support which shall steady the end of the thread, and then moves its head rather slowly, and the gummy fluid, constantly forced through the spinneret, hardens at once into a silken thread which the caterpillar guides to any point it chooses. As we watch the spinning it looks as if the caterpillar were making lines with its tongue. It is not true, as was stated in one popular book, that "whenever" the caterpillar moves its head from side to side it is spinning. It often moves the head to find another leaf or stem to which it may crawl.   Young caterpillars often spin single threads to guide them back to a starting-point or to drop from a twig without injury.

The thoracic segments of the body have the six true legs, two on each segment.   The first segment often has a horny plate across the top, or a crest of points or tubercles, and the second and third segments some-times have tubercles or marks which are more con-spicuous than those of the abdominal segments.   The second and third segments have no spiracles.

The third, fourth, fifth, and sixth abdominal seg-ments have the props or prolegs with tips, or *plan'tæ*, adapted to clinging to the stems or twigs, and the last segment has the anal props and anal plate or shield, a thick flap which covers the anus or vent.   This segment is often called the anal segment.

The spir'acles, or breathing-holes, are low down on the sides, one pair on each segment, except the second and third.

The eighth abdominal segment, which is the eleventh segment of the body, often has a horn, tubercle, or other mark more conspicuous than any on the other abdominal segments, and one soon grows used to look-ing for characteristic marks on the first three and eleventh segments.   The anal shield often has a mark around its edge or a peculiar arrangement of tubercles.   There may be thirteen segments of the body, but the last two are usually so united as to seem one.

The anal props are very thick and have a very firm grasp.

The spiracles admit air to the *tra'cheæ*, or air-tubes, in

the body of the caterpillar, which has no lungs and needs very little air to keep it healthy.

The skin of caterpillars is chitinous and is harder and stiffer on the segments than between them. It is called an exoskeleton, or outside skeleton. It is cast several times, most caterpillars molting four times, a few less often, and some oftener. Ten molts are the largest number so far observed in any species. Before molting, a caterpillar stays quiet, with its anal props firmly grasping its support, and does not eat for a day or two. Its head-cover, or mask, is pushed forward by the larger one which is rapidly forming beneath it, until it looks almost like a nose-bag fastened on the new head. When ready to cast the old skin the caterpillar begins to squirm, contracting and expanding its body in a queer way; then the skin bursts near the head and the caterpillar crawls out of it, pushing the old skin back by means of this muscular contraction and expansion. A fluid has been secreted between the old skin and the new, which enables the caterpillar to push the old skin off without harming the new skin. Not only is the skin cast in molting, but the membrane lining the intestines and spiracles is cast at the same time. The mask sometimes is pushed off when the caterpillar is partly out of the old skin, sometimes is retained until the crawler has rested after the effort of molting, and once in a while declines to be removed by any efforts of the caterpillar; we have had to take it off in order to enable the larva to eat. The new head is very large after each molt, as after hatching, but the body soon grows up to it, and then becomes larger in proportion before the next molt. Many caterpillars always eat the cast skin, with the exception of the mask.

At molting-times caterpillars are delicate and should not be disturbed or touched if this can be avoided. The early molts, especially, seem to be critical periods, and more caterpillars die then than at any other time in the history of a brood indoors. Of course out of doors many are killed by birds, squirrels, mice, toads, snakes, and so forth, and stung by parasitic flies.

After the last molt the caterpillar increases in size more rapidly than before, and eats voraciously. When full grown and ready to pupate, it stops eating, stays quiet for a day or so, and then begins crawling about as if in great haste to find a suitable place in which to spin or burrow. Usually its colors change somewhat, some larvæ growing pink on the back, others lead-colored, while others merely grow duller and the marks look faded out. The caterpillar empties its intestine, generally before it begins the rapid crawling, and in some cases the almost fluid discharge is one of the first indications of approaching pupation.

Very few caterpillars have just the same marks and colors when they come from the egg and when they are ready to pupate. Most of them pass through one or more changes of appearance in the course of their molts, and usually are more elaborately marked in the later stages. The changes of appearance through which the individual caterpillar passes between egg and pupa are thought to show the forms through which the species has passed in the course of its evolution from the original form.

The skin of a caterpillar may be smooth, rough or

granulated, or hairy, or have tubercles or warts from which grow stiff spines or bristles. In a few instances the hairs or spines are charged with a poisonous fluid secreted by glands at their base, and affect one's hands as nettles do on slight contact. The effect is short-lived, however, and leaves no ill result. The spines of *Hyperchir'ia i'o* and the hairs of *Lago'a crispa'ta* have this nettling or urticating power, and the caterpillars should be handled with care.[1]

Some caterpillars have little sacs, like pockets, which they turn inside out with a jerk when disturbed. The sacs are filled with a fluid which is in some way unpleasant to birds and other enemies, and serves to protect the larva from them, as it is thrown out by the jerking of the sac. Others protrude fine threads or filaments which discharge a defensive fluid, which may or may not have an odor perceptible to us.

The caterpillar stage is usually a little more than five weeks for species which pass the winter as pupæ or in the egg. Those which hibernate as larvæ have a much longer caterpillar life, though most of it is inactive. The *Cos'sidæ*, or boring caterpillars, which live inside the wood of trees, have still longer lives, some of them having a larva stage of three years, it is thought. We have had broods most of which fed for a month, then pupated, while one or two of the caterpillars fed for a week or two longer, and we had one brood of *cynthia* the greater number of which fed for thirty-seven days, while fifteen or twenty fed for one

---

[1] The hairs of the larvæ of the "brown-tailed moth," now established in eastern Massachusetts, cause more lasting discomfort than those of any of our native caterpillars.

hundred and five days. Generally the specimens which pass through their stages with normal rapidity are more vigorous than the slower ones.

One or two writers have claimed that the sex of a caterpillar can be regulated by the amount of food given it, abundance producing females and semi-starvation males. We have made extensive experiments with several species of caterpillars, and the result has always been that the scantly fed produced as many females, in proportion, as the full fed. The sex of the caterpillar is fixed when the caterpillar is hatched, but cannot be determined without dissection. Being immature, the caterpillar cannot reproduce its kind. Its organs of reproduction are not developed.

The "whole duty" of a caterpillar is to eat and live to grow up, and some caterpillars have to eat enough to sustain life not only in the larva and pupa stages, but in the imago stage as well, for many moths have no means of taking food. Their mouth-parts are not complete or developed.

The caterpillar contains the buds which will develop into the organs of the moth or imago. Even the wings are present as little folds or pockets in the skin, and it is in the pupa stage chiefly that these imaginal buds grow into the organs which will be of use to the moth, while the props and various organs which were of use to the caterpillar but would be useless to the moth are destroyed.

III

COCOON, PUPA, AND MOTH

PUPATION, or the act of becoming a pupa, is out-
wardly much like molting. The caterpillar stops
eating, stays quiet for a day or so, empties its intestines,
and crawls about rapidly in search of a place to spin
its cocoon, or to burrow in the earth or in soft wood,
according to the habit of its species.

Cocoons vary much in size, shape, plan of construc-
tion, and texture, and different shapes, sizes, and tex-
tures may be found even among the cocoons of the
same species.

The larvæ which burrow in the earth do so by pushing the dirt aside with their heads, making no pile at
the mouth of the burrow, but apparently packing the
dirt solid as they advance. When a caterpillar has
gone as far down as it wishes, it pushes the earth on
all sides with its head until it has made a little cave
or cell large enough to turn in, and with no passage
to the air. In this cell it lies, growing shorter
as the changes go on under the skin, and exuding a
rather gummy fluid which is absorbed by the earth
and keeps it from crumbling down on the larva,
although we have never found a cell which could be
taken out of the earth unbroken. We have tried many

2

experiments with such larvæ and their cells, and made many observations, because some writers call these cells "cocoons," but in only one cell which we have seen — and we have examined many of many species — has there been any trace of silk, and in none any cohesion of the earthen walls of the cell which justifies that name. Such as we have seen have been no more like cocoons than is the hole a toad makes in the earth, when it presses the walls of the hole smooth and firm by moving around in it.

Some caterpillars burrow in rotten or soft wood, even in hard wood, or into pithy stems, fastening themselves in by spinning a door of silk across the entrance-hole, while others spin loose webs of silk, like fish-nets, among the fallen leaves on the ground.

In these different shelters the caterpillars lie until the pupa is formed in each, when the next change is that which shall free the pupa from the now useless larva-skin. The pupa presses against the head end of the skin, and contracts and expands its body, as in molting, until the skin bursts at the head end and is cast as in molting; it may be found in a neat little wad in the bottom of a cocoon, or longer, moist, perhaps inflated, in a cell, like a garment laid aside. In both cases the skin has burst near the head, the head itself often splitting down the median suture, and the pupa has wriggled out as a soft, green, shapeless mass, which soon settles into its pupa shape, becomes firmer and brown, and is covered with a thin varnish formed by the hardening of the fluid which was secreted between the larva-skin and the pupa and enabled the pupa to push off the skin — "greased the ways," as it were.

In this shape the pupa lies until its time comes to let loose the imago — the moth. But before this time comes many changes have occurred within the brown pupa-skin. All the old organs which were necessary to the crawling, voracious caterpillar, but are not needed by the moth, must be destroyed, and this destruction is accomplished by the *phag'ocytes*, or lymph-corpuscles. The unnecessary organs are weakened from ceasing to perform the functions which they did perform in the caterpillar, and therefore are easily destroyed by the phagocytes, while the imaginal buds which are to grow into organs needed by the moth — and such organs as perform their functions during the changes from caterpillar to moth — are too strong to be harmed by the phagocytes, and are thought to be nourished by them. Such destruction of unneeded organs occurs in the caterpillar stage as well as in the pupa stage. It is probable that whenever a tissue or organ becomes unnecessary it is destroyed in this way. Investigations have shown that the organs of the moth are not fully developed in the pupa until it is nearly time for the moth to emerge, but the development is rapid when it once begins.

Some pupæ have special organs which help emergence. *Dryocampa rubicunda*, a pupa formed underground, has on its abdominal segments, at almost right angles to the body, rows of spines which keep the pupa from slipping back while working its way to the surface of the earth. The pupa must come to the surface because the soft, moist moth would be unable to make its way through the earth without injury. The pupa of *Cressonia juglandis* has two points on the top of its head, like little wedges, to open a way through the earth.

The pupæ of larvæ which spin cocoons have one means of helping the moth to emerge. Most, if not all, of them have one or more little hooks on the tip of the abdomen, which catch in the silk of the cocoon and hold the pupa-skin firmly in place so that the moth can crawl out without carrying the pupa-skin too.

The triangular tip of the abdomen of the pupa is called the *cremaster*, and corresponds to the anal, also called the *sur-anal*, plate of the caterpillar.

The moths themselves have various means of forcing an opening in the cocoons. Some have rough spines or knobs on their heads with which they cut the silken threads until they can push through them. Some have on their shoulders strong spines with five or six teeth, like saws, and cut their way through the cocoon with these. Others moisten the silk with a fluid secreted in the mouth, and acid enough to soften or dissolve the silk. We have often known that a moth was about to emerge by finding the end of the cocoon wet, and several times we have saved the life of the moth by opening the cocoon and taking the moth out when the fluid failed to serve its purpose, as sometimes happens. Either there is not enough of it or it lacks acid, and in this case the poor moth dies in its cocoon unless some one rescues it. We have found cocoons each containing a much-broken pupa-skin, a dead moth, and from sixty to two hundred eggs, these being laid all over the pupa-skin and the inside of the cocoon, showing that the moth had turned inside it and crawled all over every part of the walls, for the eggs were as carefully gummed to their support as if the moth had laid them on twigs or leaves, as she would have done had she been able to emerge from the cocoon. Of course these eggs were useless, as the moth had not mated.

The attacine moths, *cecropia, gloveri, promethea*, and *angulifera*, leave one end of the outer cocoon open and spun with long filaments which cover the opening, while the end of the inner cocoon is open, but so spun that it looks like the top of a bag gathered in "puckers" by a draw-string. There is no draw-string in the cocoon, however, and the emerging moth needs no cutter or fluid, but has only to push through the opening, whose "puckers" straighten out under the pressure, giving ample room for the moth to crawl out. It is because the silk is so broken into short lengths that it cannot be reeled from the cocoon in threads long enough to be of any commercial value as silk.

Once free from the cocoon, or the pupa-skin, the moth scrambles about until it finds a stem, stick, or the side of a box or house — something which offers a surface up which it can crawl. At this time the moth looks all head, body, and legs, with very small wings like soft, limp, moist flaps dangling from its thorax, a great contrast to the fully developed insect. Having crawled up the support as far as it wishes to go, the moth hangs by its feet with the wings down, moving its abdomen as if it were pumping fluid from it into the wings. Whether or not this pumping motion has anything to do with the expansion of the wings we have not been able to learn, but in any case the pressure of the blood causes the wings to stretch out longer and wider, as well as thinner, until they have reached their normal size and shape, after which the moth waves them gently as if to dry them, and in a few hours they are stiff and ready for flight.

Meanwhile the moth exercises its legs, rubs its antennæ, uncoils and coils its tongue, if it has one, and seems to be preparing every part for use. Later, if it is a female, it thrusts out of the end of its abdomen the ovipositor, or egg-placer, usually a yellowish, short tube, and is ready for mating.

In confinement different species of attacine moths can be expected to emerge at regular hours of the day, and ours seldom have varied much from those hours. For instance, the large attacine moths usually have come out between seven o'clock in the morning and noon, *cecropia* pretty regularly between nine and ten o'clock, and *promethea* a little earlier. These moths do not feed, and, in our experience, the females do not fly until the need of egg-laying forces them to do so. They have a strong odor — "a regular menagerie smell," it has been called — which enables the males to find them as they hang from the twigs out of doors, or the side of the cage indoors. This odor is diffused all through the day and is carried by the air to great distances, so that by the time the males begin to fly some are pretty sure to be attracted by it, follow it up, flying against the wind, and find the female. We ourselves have often found *cecropia* by following the odor. The hour of emergence cannot be said to be always the same, however, for one or two *cecropias* have come out in the afternoon in our boxes, and one emerged in the evening, and *promethea* at two in the afternoon. *Promethea* has been more regular, and the males begin to fly by three o'clock in the afternoon, and are so common that one female often attracts thirty or forty males.

The sphingid moths are less to be depended upon, emerging at almost any time between dawn and midnight. These moths have tongues, some very long ones, and fly for food, some at dusk, some later, and a few species in broad daylight. They have little or no odor perceptible to us, and we think that this is because both sexes fly to the same kinds of flowers for the nectar upon which they feed, and the males meet the females in this way without needing any odor to guide them. This is a theory of ours which we have not seen advanced by others, and we give it as a theory although convinced that it is a fact.

As the whole duty of the caterpillar is to eat and live to grow up, so the whole duty of the moth is to reproduce its kind. To do this male and female must mate, and the female must lay her eggs. Moths which fly in the daytime usually mate in the sunshine, and the dusk-flying and night-flying moths mate after sunset. In most cases they remain mated for several hours, rest quiet awhile, and then the female begins to oviposit, or lay her eggs. Egg-laying is not a short process. The eggs are growing in the body of the moth, and as they ripen they must be disposed of whether they are fertile or not. Near the end of the abdomen is the little pouch which receives the spermatozoa in mating, and, as an egg passes the opening of this pouch on its way to the ovipositor, the pressure forces one or more spermatozoa out of the pouch, one enters the micropyle of the egg, and this now fertile egg is laid by the ovipositor on a twig, leaf, or other safe place to which it is fastened by a sticky fluid which is forced out of the ovipositor with it and hardens as glue does. All moths, however, do not fasten their eggs to a support, but some drop them anywhere on the ground, or in our boxes. Such moths usually lay many eggs, and we had one *Arctia* which dropped in one of our boxes 1395 tiny yellow eggs, so small that it was a task to count them. We speak of eggs being laid "in a safe place," but they are by no means always safe. Birds often find them and eat them, and some parasitic flies pierce the shells with their ovipositors and lay their eggs inside the moth eggs. In this case the fly-larvæ devour the contents of the moth eggs, and flies hatch instead of caterpillars. Egg-laying continues for several nights, the number of eggs laid being greatest on the first night, usually, and growing smaller each night after. We had one moth which laid eggs for ten nights, and this is the greatest number our records show. It sometimes happens that a captured moth will not oviposit the first night or even the second, but afterward lays a goodly number of fertile eggs.

Probably out of doors moths usually mate before the female begins ovipositing, but in confinement it often happens that males are not at hand, and the pressure of the ripest eggs compels egg-laying. In such cases mating has sometimes taken place after one or two nights of egg-laying, when males have emerged in our cages or been attracted from out of doors. Some moths are polygamous.

Much has been written by persons who seem to think that nature is not interesting enough as it exists and that they can improve it by inventing "sweet and touching incidents" about the "unerring instinct" and the "mother-love" of moths, which cause them to choose for laying their eggs only such places as will be suitable for the young caterpillars to live in, and much emphasis has been laid on the care with which these motherly moths fasten their eggs securely in these suitable places. It all sounds very fine until one knows that the unmated moth is just as careful in laying her unfertilized eggs which can never give any caterpillars, and that mated moths often lay their eggs on plants whose leaves the caterpillars will not eat even if starving, and sometimes on stone posts, blinds, window-shades, fences, and other things not at all suitable for food for caterpillars. Observation will convince any one that egg-laying is not a matter of volition on the part of the moth, but a function which she must perform when the eggs are ready to be laid, and that by the time her eggs are all laid — often before all are laid — the moth dies, having never seen one of her offspring. It is therefore arrant nonsense to talk of the "mother-love" of a moth.

The moth, like the caterpillar, is made up of three sections, the head, the thorax, and the abdomen, with their appendages. The head carries the antennæ, or feelers, which contain the organs of smell and touch and often those of hearing. It has also the mouthparts, which may be completely developed or only partly so. If the moth feeds it has a tongue, sometimes three inches long, which it thrusts into flowers, and through whose hollow tube it sucks the nectar. The tongue is formed by the two maxillæ, which are grooved on the inner side and are so held together that the two grooved sides form a tube through which fluids may be sucked, for moths suck the juices of fruit, water, and the liquid of decaying animal matter, as well as nectar. The palpi lie at the outer sides of the tongue, or proboscis as it is also called. They are organs of touch, and possibly of smell also, but the use of their little sense-organs is not yet known.

The adult moth, except in one or two of the lower forms, has no mandibles.

The large, faceted eyes are easy to see, but besides these the moth has, in most cases, two ocelli on top of the head between and above the compound eyes. Experiments seem to show that even the compound eyes do not give the clear vision which we mean by sight, but that the moth sees moving objects without being conscious of their shape, and can see large objects as far distant as five feet, but not farther. This is higher power of vision than the caterpillar had, however, for that could distinguish only light and darkness.

The thorax is horny, carries the six legs and the four wings, has one pair of spiracles, and is covered with scales.

The legs are jointed, having five segments, and end in claws which enable the moth to cling to its support.

The wings are membranous sacs, with many veins running through them, and are more or less densely covered with scales of different shapes, sizes, and colors.

The front edge of the fore wing has a stout chitinous tube called the *costa*, the strongest part of the wing, as it has to meet the greatest pressure of the air.

If the two wings on the same side were not held together they would move separately and not serve their purpose as well. On the hind wing of most males there is a stiff spine which extends under the fore wing, preventing it from slipping by the hind wing. The females have a bunch of stiff bristles which serve the same purpose. This is called the *fren'ulum*. A few moths have no frenulum, but have instead a lobe extending backward from the hinder edge of the fore wing, and answering the same purpose. This lobe is called a *ju'gum*. A few have neither. A hand-lens magnifying fifteen or twenty diameters will show the scales fairly well. The wings are brittle and easily broken, but it requires much destruction of wing surface to disable the moth so that it cannot fly. The wing muscles are very strong, as may be proved by holding a sphinx moth by the fore wings and feeling the force of its struggle to free itself.

The females of some moths have the wings hardly developed enough to show, and never fly, but stay near the spot where they emerge, often laying their eggs on the cocoons from which they came.

On top of the thorax, near the head, are two small flaps, usually densely covered with scales, called the *pata'gia*. They seem to have no use now, but are often very ornamental. They are movable and may be erected.

The very soft abdomen is plainly divided into segments, while the divisions of the thorax are not seen plainly unless the scales are removed.   The abdominal spiracles are protected by the scales, but often may be seen clearly, two on each segment.   The last segment has the ovipositor of the female, or the claspers and intromittent organ of the male.   The claspers are horny plates with which the male holds the abdomen of the female while mating.   The intromittent organ, or ejaculatory duct, conveys the seminal fluid of the male into the pouch of the female.

Some species of moths have the power of thrusting out tufts of bristles which give an odor.   In some cases the odor is disagreeable to birds, mice, and bats, and serves to protect the moth from their attacks.   In other cases the males only possess scent-tufts, and emit an odor which is thought to be attractive to the females.   In some species the tufts are on one pair of the legs, in others on the abdomen and are concealed when not in use.   Some species have on the wings large scent-glands under the scales, others protrude long filaments which give out the odor.

In many species the male and female differ in color or marks and may be distinguished at a glance.   In others the width of the antennæ and size of the abdomen are distinguishing marks, the wider or more pectinate antennæ showing the male, while the much larger abdomen shows the female.   In other cases the different forms of the frenulum will tell the sex, while the claspers always show the male.   In entomological writings the sign ♀ is used to indicate the female, and ♂ to indicate the male.

IV

CARE OF EGGS, CATERPILLARS, AND MOTHS

HAVING eggs, the question is how to take care of them. Again the popular book is wrong when it states that "eggs must be kept in just the conditions of heat, light, and moisture in which they were found." The best and safest way of keeping them is to put them in a little circular tin box, each kind by itself, marking the box with a name or a number which shows exactly what the eggs are, or refers to the page of the note-book which tells where they were found. The little tin boxes which country druggists use for dispensing ointments are excellent egg-boxes. Better still are the boxes made in Germany with glass in the top, because in these the eggs can be watched without opening the box. Round boxes are better than square-cornered ones because they have no chinks through which the newly hatched larvæ can escape; and it is surprising to find how small a hole or crack is large enough for the loss of a whole brood of caterpillars just from the egg. In a round box, then, the eggs should be put, a bit of the thinnest scrim should be laid over the top, and the cover should be shut tight. The eggs should be examined daily to note any changes of color which may occur and to prevent the

29

possibility of the hatchlings' lacking food when they need it. This is all the care needed by eggs — except to keep the boxes out of the sunlight, as caterpillar-boxes should be kept, and in a cool place.

No parasitic flies can enter such tin boxes so closed, and this means one danger escaped by the eggs. Moreover, such boxes are too small to be likely to be seized by other members of the family for uses of their own, as once happened to an egg-box of a little girl who, when asked if her *cecropia* eggs had hatched, said: "I don't know. I had them in a nice big paste-board box, and my sister Angela wanted something to pick cherries in, so she took my box, and then she ate up all the cherries and the eggs with them"!

When the caterpillars hatch they may be put into boxes a little larger than the egg-boxes — still round ones, with scrim on top, young and tender leaves in-side, and the cover shut tight over the scrim. The leaf or leaves should be sprinkled, for the little crawlers like water. / It is a good plan not to move them from the egg-box until it is certain that they do not mean to eat any more shell. They never nibble the egg-shells after eating leaf-pulp.

Crowding is sure to be fatal to some of the larvæ if it is allowed, even when they are small. Many small caterpillars spin threads of silk as they crawl, and if there are too many in a box the little larvæ become entangled in the threads or crawl over one an-other, spinning as they crawl, and so hurt one another. In the early molts they are usually most delicate and need watching, plenty of room, and no handling. As they grow larger they need more room and older leaves, with stems or twigs to rest on, and all through the caterpillar life the leaves should be sprinkled a little.

We soon learned that leaves did not keep fresh half a day in open or pasteboard boxes; we found that bottles of water in cages or boxes were a source of danger to the caterpillars and a trouble to us; so reasoning that plants would keep fresh a long time in closed tin boxes, and that caterpillars needed very little air, we tried the experiment of putting our sprays of leaves into water for an hour or two (as we should put flowers we meant to send away in boxes), and then putting them into our larva-tins for the caterpillars to eat, or into our big tin boxes to be kept till needed. We watched our first tins of caterpillars very closely, and soon satisfied ourselves that the crawlers certainly grew as fast and as large as when in the open air, while the leaves kept far fresher than in bottles of water in open boxes or cages. Moreover, no parasitic flies can sting them in these tins, unless they are put in with the leaves, and this chance is very small. We believe we have had one instance of it, and only one. The tin boxes protected the caterpillars from mice also, while in more than one case our "best specimen" had fallen a victim to mice when we used cages or netted boxes. Another advantage of the use of tin boxes, outside of the Crawlery, is that no one is disturbed by seeing the crawlers, and there is no fear of finding caterpillars "all over the house," for none can lift the tin covers except the big tomato- or potato-caterpillars when in boxes shallow enough to let them stand with their anal props on the bottom and their heads against the cover. We have once had a boxful of these caterpillars escape in this way. Luckily we found them before any one else saw them, and since then we have always put them in deep boxes with a rubber band around each to hold the cover down, and have had no further trouble. Even in summer boarding-houses and hotels no one objects to our having caterpillars kept in this way. Its safety is recognized.

Caterpillar-tins need to be cleaned out at least once a day, and it is a good plan to have an empty tin — a " saltines " box, for instance — into which the caterpillars may be put while their box is made clean and fresh twigs or leaves are supplied. A bristle paint-brush about half an inch wide, with a handle eight or ten inches long, is a great help in cleaning the boxes. If the excrement is very soft, a little sand on the bottom of the box keeps it much cleaner.

The piece of scrim over the top of the box should be large enough to hang down on all sides for half an inch or more. We found that we occasionally beheaded a caterpillar, in putting on the box-cover, before we used scrim, but we have had no trouble since. With several very lively crawlers in a large box it is difficult to be sure that all are safely out of harm's way, especially since some species are much excited by light and crawl toward it very fast. The scrim keeps them away from the edge and saves some lives.

Leaves should not be left in the tins after they begin to lose their freshness, or after the caterpillars have eaten a part and abandoned them. Fresh food and plenty of it, a few drops of water, clean tins, and no crowding are the essentials.

Diseased or feeble larvæ should be put into separate tins, when they often recover.

A caterpillar should never be removed from the leaf or twig, but the piece it is on should be replaced in the box. The larva will crawl off to a fresh twig when ready, and then will not be injured by handling. Some books tell of the toughness of the caterpillar-skin, but slight experience will show that often a very gentle pull is enough to break the skin and kill the crawler.

Abundance of food should be provided, for the caterpillars do not over-eat, though they eat voraciously when nearly full fed. If leaves give out, the stronger sometimes eat the weaker inhabitants of the box, and we have known some of the arctians to eat freshly formed pupæ of their own kind even when leaves abounded. For this reason, and also to prevent any unintentional injury, a caterpillar about to pupate should be put into a box by itself — a spinner into a pasteboard or wooden box with scrim over the top under the cover, to prevent the cocoon's being fastened to the cover and sides of the box, and thus being torn when the box is opened. A burrowing larva may be put into an empty tin box and shut up, when in a few days the pupa will be found well formed, unless there has been some defect or disease in the larva. A few caterpillars, however,— *Protoparce celeus*, *P. carolina*, and *Ceratomia amyntor*,— exude so much gummy fluid that they need a little earth in the tin to absorb it, otherwise they may die instead of pupating. An inch of earth in the box is enough.

Pupæ should not be handled while soft, for their

3

covering is very tender and easily broken, and a break, even if it does not kill the pupa, results in a deformed moth.

Pupæ may be kept through the winter in tin boxes filled with cut sphagnum or swamp-moss, slightly moistened. The boxes should be kept away from sun and heat, yet not in freezing temperature. They should be shut and perhaps tied to keep mice and meddlers from their contents. We like sphagnum better than sawdust or earth, but all are used by entomologists, and all should be baked to kill any living creatures which might harm the pupæ. Earth should be sifted through a fine sieve. Pupæ may be kept very successfully also on an inch or two of earth which has been baked, then moistened a little, with sphagnum laid loosely over the pupæ, and room enough allowed at the top for moths to spread their wings if they emerge sooner than expected.

We have wooden boxes with glass set in the lid, wire-netting bottoms, and a thin lace over the top under the glass. We like these boxes when the time for emergence is near, for the moths can crawl up the wooden sides to the lace over the top and under the lid, and can be seen when they emerge. But such boxes are not mouse-proof. Mice, spiders, beetles, ants, birds, squirrels, snakes, toads, parasitic flies, and wasps are to be regarded as enemies to caterpillars, most of them to pupæ, and some of them to moths, which are often eaten by bats also. Skunks will eat pupæ. Cocoons may be kept in similar boxes without earth, moss, or sawdust.

When a moth emerges it is sometimes desirable to

remove it to a cage for mating, or for developing merely, and this may be done by thrusting one's finger under its legs from the front, and gently detaching it from the lace or wood. Usually the moth will crawl up the finger, but occasionally it will flop down on the bottom of the box and jerk its soft wings. In this case a bit of cloth or netting may be put near its feet, and usually the moth will cling to it, when it may be lifted and put into the cage.

A little care is necessary in approaching newly emerged moths, for when disturbed they often eject a pinkish fluid which stains cloth and probably contains acid.

If the newly emerged moth is wanted for a specimen it should be killed before it flies, as flying will rub off scales, but it will not make a good specimen if killed before it is perfectly dry and developed.

We began by using a cyanide-bottle to kill the few specimens we cared to keep, but we did not like the results very well and experimented with chloroform. This is good for small moths, but large ones are likely to revive later, and we have seen a moth pinned to a setting-board — not ours, we are glad to say — revive enough to lay eggs, though held fast by the pin, and with the wings fastened down by strips of paper. That condemned chloroform, and we tried naphtha, or gasolene, with excellent results. We use a glass pipette with a rubber bulb at one end, such as are sold for medicine-droppers and "fillers" for stylographic pens. Two or three charges of naphtha applied to the thorax and abdomen of the biggest moth we have killed, *cecropia*, kill it quickly. As soon as the moth is dead an insect-pin should be thrust through the middle of the thorax, and the moth should be pinned to a cushion or box-edge to dry.   The naphtha makes it look wet and black or discolored, but it soon evaporates, leaving the colors unchanged, and, we think, keeping the specimens free from museum pests.

When dry enough to be fluffy where the scales are long, the moth should be pinned to a setting-board, and the wings spread in a position which shows the markings and held in place by strips of smooth paper pinned across them.   The antennæ and legs must be arranged, and the abdomen supported by a bit of paper, cork, or card held fast by a pin.   If the tongue is to be shown it must be uncoiled and extended.   A pin will hold it out if the tip of the tongue is allowed to coil around it.

The setting-board is a strip of soft wood wide enough to more than hold the outspread wings, and having through the middle, lengthwise, a groove deep and wide enough to hold the body of the moth.   This groove should have a thin strip of cork on the bottom for the points of the insect-pins.   It is evident that boards of several sizes will be needed.

Moths should be left to dry on the setting-board for about two weeks, and then will be very brittle, needing most careful handling to prevent legs and antennæ from breaking off.   While the moths are drying it is well to put the board into a tin box or case of some kind where they cannot be reached by any insect pest.   If left uncovered, clothes-moths and buffalo-beetles may lay eggs on them, and even naphtha might not save them.

If wanted for eggs the female moth must be mated.

This is easy, if there happens to be a male out at the same time or even a day later; they have only to be put into the same cage. But sometimes no male is at hand, and one must be attracted. This may be managed in two ways. The female may be put in a cage with a wire-netting top and set out at night, or dusk, in a suitable place. For feeding moths a suitable place is one near the kind of flowers to which these moths fly for food. Any males flying there will flutter about the cage and may be caught by the watching entomologist and put into the cage, when mating will probably take place before morning. This prevents all danger from bats, owls, and early birds, but is not always convenient for the entomologist.

The other way is to tie a soft but strong string around the thorax of the moth between the fore and hind wings, and fasten the other end to a bush or tree in such wise as to give the moth a short flight and a leafy branch to hide under. If birds and bats fail to find her the result is usually successful. In the case of the non-feeding species, the large attacine moths for instance, there is no need of going in search of favorable places, unless one lives in a city and not near a garden or park. The moth may be tied out of the window, given a spray of leaves to conceal it from the birds, and will be almost sure to be found mated in the morning, if in a place where its species is found. It is well to rise before " the lark," however, when one has moths tied out, for birds, especially the English sparrows, are prying creatures and interfere with one's best arrangements of this kind, and it is necessary to forestall them.

If mating moths are found they can be taken in the fingers, gently, and put into a cage with their feet on the netting, usually without disturbing them. In any case the female should be held, since she is the source of the egg-supply.

Sphingid moths do not remain mated as long as bombycid moths, and are not as likely to be found together in the morning. Finding a female alone does not necessarily mean that she has not mated. Most captured females will be fertile, but if one is found which is evidently fresh from the pupa it will need mating.

Mating-cages can be made of paper or wooden boxes having four uprights extending five or six inches above the top of the box. The netting cover which forms the cage may be of wire or of lace, cut to fit, and fastened to the box by tacks or a rubber band. With wire netting it is easier to have half the top made to open to admit moths. Most moths dart downward when disturbed. With the lace or mosquito-netting cage the edge can be pushed up enough to admit the moth. A small salt-box makes a good cage for medium-sized moths. So does a pound candy-box, while a starch-box makes a palatial cage for the largest *cecropia*. Tin boxes give a moth no foothold and are not good

When a moth begins to oviposit she should be put in a paper box with lace over the top (old veils are excellent for moth-boxes). This is for the purpose of detaching the eggs easily. The lining of a paper box can be cut off with a sharp knife, while it is difficult to remove eggs from a wooden or tin box without breaking them.

In order to know the lives of the crawlers, exact notes must be kept, and nothing trusted to memory. The box of eggs should be numbered to correspond with a page in the note-book. On this page should be written the date when the eggs were laid, a description of the eggs and whether they were laid singly, in rows, in a mat, or encircling a stem; the date of hatching; whether or not the larvæ ate the shells; any other habits observed; and a full description of the young caterpillars. The boxes containing the caterpillars, as they are divided after removal from the egg-box, should be given the same number, and the note-book page should have the name as well if it is known.

The record of the caterpillars' life should give the food-plant chosen, the dates of molts, full descriptions of the larvæ after each molt, habits, degree of voracity, and any other characteristics observed. It should be noted when the caterpillars stopped eating before pupation, when the spinning or burrowing began, and when the pupa cast the larva-skin, and the pupa should be fully described and then given the same number as the larva.

Where the kinds of pupæ can be kept in separate boxes, each box can be numbered like the larva-tins of the species, but where several species must be kept in one box the box should be numbered or lettered, and a list of the contents of "Box 1" or "Box A" entered in a note-book. In this case care must be taken not to put into the same box pupæ of species so similar as to make any doubt as to which moth emerges from which pupa or cocoon. For instance, if we had two

small sphingid pupæ which we were not able to identify, we put them in different boxes, to be sure which
pupa gave which moth.

Caterpillars found out of doors should be described,
numbered, and recorded in the same way, unless they are
so well known that no notes are needed. In recording
a brood of caterpillars one box should be selected, and
the dates given should be those of the first specimens
to hatch, molt, pupate, etc., that the record may be
true of the length of individual stages. The eggs laid
the first night usually hatch first, and the first caterpillars usually pass through their stages normally,
while those from the last eggs vary more. This may
not be a recognized rule, but we have found it to be
the case in many instances.

To pack living caterpillars for transportation from
one place to another, a tin box of suitable size should
be chosen. It should be a stout tin, not easy to bend
or dent. Into this should be put as many twigs and
leaves of the food-plant as it will hold, after they have
been in water for an hour or two. Putting the twigs
in water, like flowers, keeps their leaves fresh for the
journey. The caterpillar, or caterpillars, should be
put in among the twigs, and the box closed over a bit
of scrim and wrapped in heavy brown paper. *There
should never be any holes in the box or paper.* We have
sent hundreds in this way without any injury.

Living moths may be sent in tin or wooden boxes
with a twig to which they can cling, but they often
die by the way. We have received moths, sent in this
way, apparently dead, and have had them revive when
the box was opened and air admitted. Spread speci-

mens of dead moths should be packed in a cork-lined box, and this box put into a larger one, with loose crushed paper, excelsior, or hay between the two boxes.

Eggs may be sent in quills with the ends stopped with cotton, in hollowed cork, or in flat tin boxes. If there is any chance of their hatching on the way, tin boxes with leaves should be used. Quills sometimes break under pressure, and are not as safe as tins. A tin bean-shooter cut into two-inch lengths is better than quills, though not always as easy to get.

Pupæ should be rolled separately in strips of damp cotton cloth and packed very carefully in substantial boxes.

V

HUNTING

TO the uninitiated, hunting for moths' eggs seems like looking for a needle in a hay-mow, but it is a much more successful performance. We have often found eggs of *Hyperchiria io* on beach-plum; of *Actias luna* and *Telea polyphemus* on the twigs or leaves of white birch; of *Attacus promethea* on wild cherry, willow, tulip-tree; of *Lagoa crispata* on bayberry or beach-plum; of *Limacodes scapha* on bayberry; of *Protoparce carolina* and *Protoparce celeus* on tomato; of *Ampelophaga myron*, *Thyreus abbotii*, *Amphion nessus*, and *Deilephila inscripta* on woodbine; of *Anisota stigma* and *Anisota senatoria* on oak; of *Ceratomia undulosa* on fringe-tree or lilac; of *Sphinx chersis* on fringe-tree, ash, or lilac; and of other species on their special food-plants. With sharp eyes, patience, and a little knowledge of where to look and for what to look, the results are sometimes very surprising, though of course the easiest way to get eggs is to have fertile egg-layers.

Caterpillars also may be hunted successfully, and very little practice will increase the success.

Both eggs and caterpillars are protected from notice in various ways. The sphingid eggs, found on the

backs of woodbine-leaves, are of the exact shade of
green shown by the leaves, and look more like small
drops of water through which the leaf color shows
than like anything else—to the untrained eye. The
eggs of *polyphemus* are white with a brown band
around them, of just the colors of the warts or excrescences on white-birch twigs. The eggs of *D. inscripta*,
laid among the flower-buds of woodbine, are so like
these buds in size, shape, and color that a keen-eyed
doctor, a naturalist himself, told us that he thought
we had " made a mistake for once," and it needed a
magnifier and forceps to convince him that the eggs
were not buds growing in the clusters. So the young
sphingid caterpillars are usually of the exact color of
the leaves on which they rest and feed, but they may
be traced by tiny holes through the leaf, then by
ragged bites on the edges of the leaf, and as they grow
larger by bare midribs and stems. Holes through the
leaves are not a sure sign of caterpillars, however, for
some are made by beetle-larvæ, and clean semicircles
cut from leaf-edges mean leaf-cutter bees. Eyes are
soon trained to distinguish, and a certain unconscious
knowledge comes to the caterpillar-hunter — an intui-
tion, not the result of any conscious process of thought
or reasoning. To the caterpillar-hunter, " What has
been eating this bush?" is not slang, but a question of
importance and great interest. Larger caterpillars are
protected in different ways. Some resemble the leaves
and twigs among which they live, and their colored
marks curiously follow the changing colors of the
maturing leaves, as in *astylus* and *myops*, which are
plain green when young, but gain red marks as they

grow older and the leaves begin to show their autumnal coloring. Others have the surface color broken by lines and patches of colors unlike the leaves and twigs themselves, but resembling the effects of light and shade on them as they grow, and such larvæ blend with their surroundings in a marvelous way.

Some have eversible sacs which discharge an unpleasant fluid; others have the power of protruding horns or lashes which may or may not have a disagreeable odor. The lashes may be vibrated, as *Cerura* vibrates those in its "fork-tails," and terrify some of the foes that attack the caterpillar. It is thought probable that the caudal horns of the sphingid larvæ formerly held terrifying lashes, and that these have disappeared in the course of evolution, from disuse, the horn being left in most species. Others are protected from devourers, but not from entomologists, by an unpleasant taste.

Early morning and near sunset are the best times for finding caterpillars, as many kinds hide during the day and feed at night or toward dark; still, we have found hundreds in morning walks. The excrement, or droppings, of the caterpillars often betrays their hiding-place, and we have traced many by this means.

Cocoons may be found in winter on bare branches, bush-stems, tree-trunks, fences, among leaves on the ground, or spun to all sorts of supports. These may contain parasites.

Pupæ may be found in cellar-window areas, among leaves on the ground, or by digging in potato- or tomato-beds, or near trees or bushes where burrowing larvæ have fed; but these are likely to be of stung larvæ, and the most satisfactory pupæ are those reared from the egg. If alive, a pupa will squirm after being held for a while in the warm hand. Cocoons cannot be tested as easily, although if there is a heavy, solid thud when the cocoon is shaken the pupa is pretty sure to be alive. If the cocoon feels light it should be cut open, and usually will be found to contain a dried caterpillar, a package of small parasite cocoons, or one big parasite cocoon. Many cocoons are found with small holes through which parasites have escaped, and others torn or gnawed open by birds or mice which have feasted on the pupa. Even the dangling *promethea* cocoons do not always escape the birds, while the cocoons of the tent-caterpillars are rifled by thousands. Cocoon-hunting is very profitable, however, and very interesting.

Moths may be attracted by light and caught in a net. They may be attracted by sweet flowers, or by baiting a fence-rail, stump, or post with rum and molasses, rotten apples, or honey and rum. They may be caught at electric lights, or collected under them, often too much battered for specimens, but able to oviposit. The moth which gave us our life-history of *Trip'togon modes'ta*, by no means common, was picked up under a street arc-light; its wings were too much broken to fly, but it laid us one hundred and fifty eggs.

Some collectors have great success in beating bushes and saplings for moths, but we have not found this profitable. We have found many moths resting on tree-trunks, piazza-roofs, the sides of buildings, stone walls, or fences, where daylight has overtaken them without causing them to fly to hiding-places. In such cases they are easily caught — except the *Catoc'-alæ*, or "under-wing moths," so called from the bright red or yellow hind wings of many members of the family. These moths start at a shadow or slight jar and lead the pursuer a weary chase, for their fore wings are so mottled as to resemble lichens or bark with lichens on it, and make the moth almost invisible when it alights on a tree or stone, the closed fore wings covering the gay hind wings — and it alights often and suddenly.

Open sheds or carriage-shelters, the under surfaces of bridges spanning either water, roads, or tracks, and light-colored walls near electric lights, are good places for finding moths in the morning. In summer hotels, where a light burns in the white-walled halls up-stairs, with open, unscreened windows, we have taken many good and some rare moths at night. They seem to find some attraction in the intense white of the wall near the light or opposite it, and are caught very easily. This hunting must be very quiet, of course, but it is perfectly easy to do it so noiselessly that nobody knows that any one is in the hall. Lighted windows and screen doors often attract moths, which may be caught from the outside.

After all, the pleasantest hunt is that for eggs and caterpillars, for it includes a stroll along roads lined with a tangle of bushes and saplings; or following the low growth by the brook, or by the edges of the woods; or along the stone walls or rail fences, where wild cherry, poplar, birch, sassafras, viburnum, young ash, maple, oak, sweet-fern, blueberry, whortleberry, inkberry, wild grape, and woodbine grow; or among the low pines, where may be found choice sphingid larvæ, the big brown or green *Eacles imperialis* and the smaller brown *Platycerura furcilla* caterpillars. In the pastures by the sea the beach-plum, andromeda, bayberry, azalea, laurel, tupelo, all have their treasures, while willows everywhere should be examined carefully, especially low-growing bushes and sapling shoots.

Near Boston May is the earliest month for profitable caterpillar-hunting or moth-hunting, unless the last of April is very warm. Farther south the season opens earlier, but from the time it begins until cold weather ends it the procession of species never stops, though it is a bigger procession in June, July, and September, in New England, than at other times.

Many species are double-brooded, one set of eggs being laid in May or June, and the moths from these mating and ovipositing in August or September; but even of these species there are stragglers all the way between those broods. There are few species of which we should be willing to state that they appear at a certain time only. *Clisiocampa americana* and *C. disstria* we have never found as caterpillars or moths later than the middle of July, and their eggs, laid then, remain on the trees all winter, unless the creepers, woodpeckers, chickadees, nuthatches, or thrifty human beings remove them.

Caterpillars full grown and crawling on the walks or ground are usually in search of a place for pupation, so no food need be provided for them; but with those found on plants, twigs of the plant should be put into the collecting-box, that the hunter may know what kind of leaves to provide for each species he finds. Most species will eat more than one kind of leaves. Those which eat wild cherry will usually eat cultivated cherry, willow, apple, plum, poplar, and sometimes ash, pear, rose, tulip-tree, oak, box-elder, spiræa, and maple. Those eating grape will eat woodbine and the Japanese woodbine, while those eating hickory will usually eat butternut and black walnut as well.

Pao'nias excœca'tus eats poplar, white birch, willow, spiræa, wild cherry, hazel, apple, weigelia, oak, elm, and hickory.

We have found *Te'lea polyphe'mus* on maple, oak, poplar, willow, tulip-tree, ash, wild cherry, white birch, hop-hornbeam, apple, chestnut, and twice on pine and wild grape. It has been found on elm also.

The list of food-plants of *Apatelo'des torrefact'a* and *Halesido'ta macula'ta* would contain the names of most of the common shrubs and trees, with blackberry and raspberry added.

When unknown caterpillars are brought in with no food we give them a choice of all the leaves we have at hand, and then supply those which they prefer. A little experience shows whether a new larva is likely to want leaves of trees, shrubs, vines, or of plantain, dandelion, and similar plants. No hard-and-fast rules for distinguishing can be given, for while sphingid caterpillars usually feed on trees, vines, and shrubs, some live chiefly on purslane, tomato, potato, tobacco, turnips; and while many hairy caterpillars live on plantain, dandelion, and the like, others live on hickory, elm, maple, and other trees. In the same way it is impossible to give one distinguishing mark for

sphingid larvæ and another for bombycids, or noto-
dontids. Most sphingid larvæ have a caudal horn at
some stage of their life, but there are species which
do not, while the notodontid *Pheo'sia rimo'sa* has a
caudal horn and smooth skin, and is usually mistaken
for a sphingid caterpillar by beginners.

We might say that of our sphingid larvæ no species
has spines or is hairy when full grown, but *Pheosia
rimosa* also is not spiny or hairy, and is not sphingid.

In this identifying caterpillars nothing helps as
much as good pictures and descriptions and a little
experience, unless one can go to a collection of blown
specimens and compare his own with these. This,
however, can seldom be done out of cities and does
not help summer work.

We are often asked how to keep specimens of moths,
and we usually answer that it depends upon one's
available space and the money he wishes to spend for
cases. There are many kinds of cabinets, cases, and
boxes at various prices, but they are not absolutely
necessary for the safe-keeping of moths. We have
two cigar-boxes with strips of cork on the bottom,
sides, and ends, in which the same specimens have
been kept for seven or eight years unharmed by anything. Of course they do not show off as well as in
handsome white-lined cases, but they have been as
safe. We have some cases also for the few specimens
we care to keep, but we find more satisfaction in
studying the living creatures than in collecting dead
moths, however beautiful.

Empty cocoons may be kept in any kind of box,
labeled.

4

Few beginners care to preserve caterpillars, and the process of making blown specimens is not attractive, though it gives better specimens than any other process. The contents of the dead caterpillar's body must be pressed out through the anus, and a small pipe must be inserted, through which the skin is inflated to its natural size, while the inflated skin must be baked in a little oven until it stiffens. Even this method does not give very satisfactory results. The blown larvæ seldom look natural, and the colors usually change, though not as much as those of specimens kept in alcohol. We much prefer photographs of the living caterpillar with its natural surroundings to these unreal-looking specimens, although we fully realize the value of the latter for other purposes than identification.

Cost need never deter any one from studying the lives of moths, for little apparatus is needed. A net can be made with a circle or ellipse of stiff wire fastened to a stick four feet long — or longer if desired — and a bag of the better quality of mosquito-netting; better still, cotton wash-lace, which makes a net cost very little, even if the hardware-dealer makes the net-frame.

Druggists, grocers, and some confectioners gladly give tin boxes which they would otherwise throw away. Many of the house supplies come in tins also — biscuits of various kinds, broma, chocolate, spices, and some brands of coffee and tea very popular in the country. Scrim costs a few cents a yard, and rubber bands are not expensive and last a long time if the right sizes are used — large enough not to be too much

stretched. Cigar-boxes and starch-boxes are easy to
get, and pasteboard boxes are gladly given away by
stationers and dry-goods dealers. Any boy or girl who
has a little knowledge of tools can make setting-boards,
the wood for which costs little. Naphtha is cheap,
and a pipette costs five cents. Chloroform costs more,
but need not be used at all, though it is sometimes
convenient. Note-books need not be expensive. Books
are the expensive item of a thorough equipment, but
much can be done without many books, and the mod-
ern public libraries usually have some entomological
books, to which one can go for information and for
some identification.

The best part of any one's equipment is the power
of observation — quick seeing, unfailing carefulness,
exactness of noticing and stating, and the patience
which works hard and well, can bear the failure of its
best plans and experiments, and begin over again next
season with as much zest as before. Faithfulness, accuracy, and patience are absolutely necessary to satisfactory work of this kind.

It is always well to rear twice as many caterpillars
as one expects to want, for some one always wants all
that can be spared. Species common in one place
may be rare in another, and it is pleasant to give
treasures to those who want them. Besides, entomologists often exchange pupæ, eggs, and larvæ, and in
this way one can sometimes obtain a species that has
been longed for but never found.

It is not very often that a whole brood of caterpillars can be reared successfully. Accident, disease,
parasites — if the larvæ were found out of doors —

usually kill some; and a margin should be allowed for such losses, for one may not have a brood of the same kind again for years.   There is as much luck in moth-hunting as in fishing, and one can never be sure of the " catch " until it is at home, so it is well to make the most of a present chance.

Even when found, caterpillars are not always " good." They may be stung by parasitic flies, and though they may live through pupation, the fly-larvæ will devour their tissues and so destroy them, and only flies will emerge.   Sometimes we find caterpillars with the white eggs of the fly on their heads or bodies. If there are not too many eggs, and if they are so fresh that the grubs have not left them and eaten their way into the caterpillar's body, we remove them with either a knife or small forceps, and the caterpillar is safe. If the eggs give a yellow liquid when crushed by the forceps, they have not hatched.   The caterpillar will squirm while under treatment, and care must be taken not to squeeze it too much or to injure its skin with the knife.   Some flies pierce the skin and lay their eggs inside the body of the caterpillar, and in this case we cannot save it or even know that it is stung.

Moreover, all one's pupæ may not live to give the moth.   Sometimes a fungus covers them and kills them.   Sometimes they dry up from some unknown cause, others in the same box being perfectly healthy. Sometimes they liquefy and decay without any apparent reason.   Taking all these possibilities into consideration, one can hardly have too many pupæ or cocoons of any kind.

It is much work to care for a large supply of caterpillars during the weeks of their feeding-time; it requires regularity, carefulness, and some exercise in keeping up the supply of leaves; but the results pay for the work, and it is all interesting.

For convenience in describing, the body of a caterpillar is mapped out in sections, each area being given a name, and the lines separating them being named also. These lines may be only imaginary, or there may be one or more of them as actual marks on the larva.

The plan of the caterpillar shows the lines which bound these areas. It is not a drawing of any real caterpillar, but merely a map or plan of caterpillar surface and appendages on one side.

The *dorsum*, or dorsal area, is the back, included between the subdorsal lines on the two sides (*y–y*). It is bisected by the dorsal line.

The *lateral area* is that bounded by the subdorsal (*y–y*) and sublateral lines (*z–z*), and is bisected by the lateral line.

The *stigmatal area* is that between the sublateral (*z–z*) and substigmatal (*s–s*) lines, and is bisected by the stigmatal line.

The *venter*, or ventral area, is that between the legs and props, extending from head to anal end, and is bisected by the ventral line. Between this area and the substigmatal line is the subventral line or area.

The most common marks on caterpillars are the dorsal line; the subdorsal line; the obliques, or oblique lines, of sphingid larvæ, often extending across two or three areas; the sublateral line, frequently present on the thoracic segments only; and the stigmatal line.

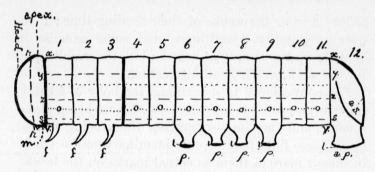

r–r, face-line; 1–12, body segments; 1, 2, 3, thoracic segments; 12, anal segment; 4–12, abdominal segments; *f,* feet or legs; *p,* props or prolegs; *a p,* anal props; *a s,* anal shield or plate; *o–o,* spiracles or stigmata; *l,* planta, or tip of prop, the grasping tip; *x–x,* dorsal line; *y–y,* subdorsal line; - - - -, lateral line; *z–z,* sublateral line; ׀ ׀ ׀, stigmatal line; *s–s,* substigmatal line; *v–v,* ventral surface; *m,* mandibles.

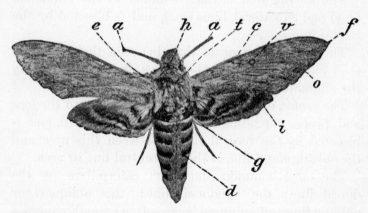

a, antennæ; *b,* collar; *c,* costa; *d,* abdomen; *e,* base of wing; *f,* apex of wing; *g,* anal angle of wing; *h,* head; *i,* inner margin of wing; *o,* outer margin of wing; *t,* thorax; *v,* discal dot.

These letters refer also to the moth on the opposite page.

The *median suture* is the line down the front of the head where two segments join. It is often mentioned in descriptions.

Horns, tubercles, and *warts* are excrescences varying in size and shape, " warts" being often used for the smallest and least conspicuous.

Granules, or *granulations,* are raised dots on the skin, giving it roughness.

Irrorations is a word used by many writers to indicate dots not as much raised or as rough as granules. We have called these simply *raised dots.*

The anal plate is also called the *sur-anal* or *supra-anal plate* or *shield,* and this is perhaps more descriptive, since it is a plate over the anus, but we have preferred the shorter word.

The parts of a moth are shown in the two figures.

Pectinate antennæ are toothed like a comb, and may have teeth so long that the antennæ look like feathers, and sometimes have more than one row of teeth.

Ciliate antennæ have short hair-like projections from their sides.

VI

PARASITES — COLLECTING

WE have stated that parasitic flies prey upon the early stages of moths, some on the eggs and some on the larvæ. Some of these flies are *Hymenop'-tera*, that is, "membrane-winged," with four clear wings, the fore wings being the larger. The females have ovipositors which can pierce an egg-shell or the skin of a caterpillar.

Thanks to the kindness of Dr. William H. Ashmead, we can give the names of the *Hymenoptera* which attack the eggs and larvæ of the *Sphing'idæ, Ceratocamp'idæ,* and *Saturni'idæ.*

Tele'nomus sphing'is, Ashm., and *Anasta'tus pear'-salli,* Ashm., pierce the eggs and lay their own eggs in them. Of course they must be very tiny flies, or their larvæ could not find in these small eggs food enough to enable them to grow up, pupate, and emerge as flies, one or more in each moth egg.

We have found mats of very small eggs on leaves, and hoped for some new crawler, only to have pieces of the shells lift and tiny black flies emerge from the whole mat, not one egg being overlooked by the busy fly-mother.

The *Hymenoptera* ovipositing in or on the caterpillars are:

> *Thyreo'don mo'rio*, Fab.
> *Enemo'tylus macru'rus*, Linné.
>   (This has been called *O'phion macru'rus*.)
> *Enemo'tylus arc'tiæ*, Ashm.
> *Ano'malon exile*, Prov.
> *Crypt'us nun'tius*, Say.
> *Cryptus extre'matus*, Cress.
> *Hemit'eles mesocho'ides*, Riley MS.
> *Hemit'eles minu'tus*, Riley MS.
> *Ameloc'tonus fugiti'vus*, Say.
> *Micropli'tis cerato'miæ*, Riley.
> *Apan'teles euchœ'tes*, Ashm.
> *Apanteles empre'tiæ*, Ashm.
> *Apanteles hemileu'cœ*, Riley.
> *Apanteles smerin'thi*, Riley.
> *Apanteles congrega'tus*, Say.
> *Heterog'amus famipen'nis*, Cress.
> *Heterogamus tex'anus*, Cress.

To the kindness of Mr. D. W. Coquillett we owe the
following names of the *Diptera*, or two-winged flies,
which attack the *Sphingidæ*, *Ceratocampidæ*, and *Saturniidæ*.

The following have been obtained from the sphingid
larvæ:

	From
Cerato'mia amyn'tor	*Stur'mia inquina'ta*, V. L. W.
Ceratomia catal'pæ	{ *Euphoro'cera claripen'nis*, Macy. { *Frontina french'ii*, Will.
Ceratomia undulo'sa	{ *Exoris'ta cerato'miæ*, Coq. { *Sturmia inquinata*, V. L. W.

Deile'phila linea'ta . . { *Sturmia inquinata*, V. L. W.
{ *Winthe'mia quadripustula'ta*, Fabr.

Hema'ris diffi'nis . . . . *Winthemia quadripustulata*, Fabr.

Philam'pelus a'chemon . *Sturmia inquinata*, V. L. W.

Philampelus vi'tis . . . *Frontina violenta*, Walk.

Protopar'ce caroli'na . . *Sturmia inquinata*, V. L. W.

Protoparce ce'leus . . { *Sturmia inquinata*, V. L. W.
{ *Sturmia distinct'a*, Wied.
{ *Winthemia quadripustulata*, Fabr.

Protoparce cingula'ta . . *Sturmia inquinata*, V. L. W.

Protoparce jamaicen'sis . *Sturmia distincta*, Wied.

Smerin'thus ceri'syi . . *Frontina frenchii*, Will.

Sphinx cher'sis . . . . *Sturmia inquinata*, V. L. W.

From the ceratocampid larvæ have been obtained:

From

Aniso'ta senato'ria . . { *Euphorocera claripennis*, Macy.
{ *Frontina frenchii*, Will.

Anisota virginien'sis . . *Frontina frenchii*, Will.

Cithero'nia rega'lis . . { *Frontina frenchii*, Will.
{ *Belvo'sia bifascia'ta*, Fabr.

Dryocamp'a rubicun'da { *Belvosia bifasciata*, Fabr.
{ *Frontina frenchii*, Will.

Sphingicamp'a bi'color . *Frontina frenchii*, Will.

From the saturniid larvæ:

From

At'tacus cecro'pia . . { *Frontina frenchii*, Will.
{ *Winthemia quadripustulata*, Fabr.

Hyperchir'ia i'o . . . { *Exorista eu'dryæ*, Town.
{ *Frontina frenchii*, Will.

Te'lea polyphe'mus . . { *Frontina frenchii*, Will.
{ *Winthemia quadripustulata*, Fabr.

From this latter list it will be seen that each parasitic fly preys upon more than one species of larva, also that almost every species of larva is victimized by more than one parasite species. It is also the case that a larva may be attacked by both *Diptera* and *Hymenoptera*, and by more than one species of each order, and it is by no means certain that we have yet found out all the species parasitic on even the well-known caterpillars and eggs. For instance, it was only in 1895 that *Apanteles congregatus*, Say, a hymenopterous fly, was recorded as attacking *Amphi'on nes'sus*, though it was well known to live upon *Ampeloph'aga my'ron*, *Dol'ba hylœ'us*, *Protoparce celeus*, *P. carolina*, *Sphinx plebe'ius*, and *Ceratomia catalpœ*. One of Us found the yellow cocoons set close together like a crust over the caterpillar's back, and sent them to Dr. Ashmead to be identified, for we had never happened to find them on any caterpillar before. Dr. Ashmead wrote that *Amphion nessus* was "a new host" for this fly.

It is a good plan to kill any flies that emerge from a pupa or larva, and keep a specimen, keeping also a record of the name of its host. This record may be numbered like the specimen. A beginner cannot know whether he has an old species or a new one, a common host or one not known as host of that fly, and some one may want that information some day. We have learned by sad experience that some of the most valuable chances come to those who do not know enough to appreciate their value and therefore fail to benefit by them.

Very early in our work, when we were studying

everything that came in our way without realizing
how much more we could really learn by confining
our study to narrower limits, One of Us brought in an
alder-branch nearly covered with cottony aphids. It
was placed in the corner of a room occupied by the
Other of Us,— for we were then in a country hotel,—
and the abundance of fresh material gathered every
day made us leave this untouched.   One day the Other
of Us said: "Do look at my pincushion!   It is all
covered with funny little cases like aces of clubs, only
not black." Examination showed them to be chrysalids, and many more were found on the walls, curtains,
and doors. They were collected and put into a box to
be kept until the following spring, but on opening the
box a few weeks later the butterflies were found dead,
having emerged in time for a second brood. We did
not know about second broods then. We knew that
the caterpillars which made the chrysalids must have
come from the alder-bough, as there was no other
source from which they could have come. We threw
away all the butterflies but three or four, and when
we next went to see an entomologist we took these to
learn their names, for our books gave nothing by
which we could identify them. He was enthusiastic
over "the rare *Fenis'eca tarquin'ius*," and asked all
sorts of questions about them, begging the butterflies
for a museum. Of course we were very sorry that we
had not known their value and kept more of them,
but we were far more sorry a few years later when
an entomologist published the life-history of the
species, showing that the little caterpillars fed wholly
upon the larvæ of the cottony aphids, a most unusual

departure from the vegetable diet of the order. Then we thought how we had had the whole story in our room, and might have discovered it all for ourselves if we had only known enough. This is a butterfly story, but we give it to show the importance of thorough, careful observation, and of keeping records and specimens of which one may not know the worth at the time.

Another lost chance was when one of our village acquaintances found a male and female *Triptogon modesta* on a fence, and chloroformed them at once. The female revived after being set on the board, and, in spite of a pin through her thorax, laid several eggs. This also was in the very early days of our study, when we were so much absorbed in getting the names of all the moths we found that we did not think of the value of these eggs until it was too late, and we were sorry enough that we lost our chance of getting the first description of the larvæ, much less known then than now, and by no means common now. We might have had the whole history from the eggs thrown away by the finder of the moths. These were the very first moth eggs we ever saw, and would have given us a "previously untold story" if we had but known enough to save them. It was twenty years before we had another chance of rearing *T. modesta* from the egg.

In almost every country or seaside place the children can be interested very easily in bringing moths, cocoons, and caterpillars to any one whom they know to want them. The village children are usually glad of a chance to earn a few cents every day or two, and the city children are eager to find all the wonders of

"the country" and to know "all about" them. They
make capital hunters, too, and to their sharp eyes we
owe many valuable caterpillars and moths. It makes
their summer much more interesting to look for specimens, and them much happier to feel that they are
really helping some one. At first they will doubtless
bring in creatures one does not care to have, the saw-
fly larva, *Cim'bex america'na,* for instance, which
abounds on elm, willow, hazel, alder, and other plants.
It may be white, yellow, salmon-pink, or green, with
two narrow black dorsal lines and twenty-two legs.
It belongs to the hymenopterous family *Tenthre-
din'idæ,* a family whose larvæ do much damage by de-
foliating trees of various kinds. The flies are called
saw-flies, because the abdomen of the female has a
pair of saws with which she saws slits in the stems or
leaves of plants, and in the slits lays her eggs. The
larvæ are not true caterpillars, but have a pair of prolegs on almost every segment of the abdomen, while
but one family of true caterpillars has more than ten
abdominal props. Another species of saw-fly lives in
large numbers on the pine, another on the white birch,
another on the rose, another on the currant, and usually there are so many together that a child thinks the
group a great treasure, and is disappointed when it is
not received with enthusiasm. Some of the saw-fly
larvæ have an unpleasant habit of discharging from
glands on their sides a disagreeable, slimy fluid. This
is their protection from birds and squirrels.

Great numbers of "woolly bears" will be brought in
late in the season. Those with white, pale yellow, and
fox-colored hairs will probably spin in the autumn, but

Cimbex americana (saw-fly).

Crœsus latitarsus (saw-fly larvæ).

Lophyrus abbotii (saw-fly larvæ).

the "double-enders"—those fox-colored in the middle
and black at both ends—hibernate, that is, pass the
winter in a torpid or semi-torpid state, and crawl out
in early spring to eat a little new grass, dandelion, or
plantain before spinning their cocoons. These are not
worth trying to keep over the winter unless one has a
room with even temperature and can have sods in a
box. In this case the caterpillars will hide in the turf
and may survive the winter, but it is difficult to keep
hibernating larvæ in ordinary heated rooms, or in cel-
lars to which many persons have access.

Whenever gipsy-moth caterpillars, apple-tree tent-
caterpillars, or forest tent-caterpillars are brought in,
or the "fall web" caterpillars or moths, they should be
destroyed, for they do much damage to the trees and
increase rapidly. This is true of the tussock-caterpil-
lars also, and of the "canker-worms," which drop down
by silken threads and hang squirming just on a level
with one's face. These are all well known and easy to
identify by books and museum specimens. When neither books nor collections can be consulted, the nearest
entomologist, the State Entomologist, or the head of the
Division of Entomology of the United States Department of Agriculture, is usually glad to give any information possible, and even beginners may be able to
repay the kindness by supplying specimens wanted for
some special purpose, or facts about some species occurring in their neighborhood.

There are more kinds, or species, of insects than of
any other class of the animal kingdom, and they are
thought to make up four fifths of that kingdom.

They are supposed to have developed from annelid

worms.   That is, ages ago some of these worms varied
from the regular type, for one of the natural laws is
that there is a tendency to vary among individuals of
the same species and even of the same brood.   As the
conditions of the earth's surface and climate changed,
those worms which had varied in ways which made
them fittest to bear these changes survived, while the
least fit died.   No one can tell how many species have
become extinct in this way.

The changed conditions caused variations in the
creatures, as well as made them necessary, and as
changes were constantly occurring, though they were
slow, new species were developed from the old forms until they reached the stages in which we see them to-day,
stages of much higher development than the worms
possess, with more complicated structure and far higher
powers.   Therefore, though a caterpillar is a crawling
creature, and though some dictionaries allow all crawling creatures to be called *worms*, it is not fair or just
to call them so.   Names like " canker-worm," " fall
web-worm," and " silk-worm " have become a part of
our language, and will be used by all sorts of writers
and in talking, but we need not perpetuate the mistake and the injustice of calling all caterpillars
" worms."

The changes from caterpillar to pupa and from
pupa to moth are called *metamorphoses*, and are
thought to have been caused originally by changes of
food, of surroundings, and of hot and cold seasons, as
well as by other changing conditions.

In order to continue the life of the species, moths
must survive the winter in some form not requiring

food. Many species pass the winter as eggs, more as torpid or semi-torpid larvæ, most as pupæ, and probably some as perfect moths, though we have not found hibernating moths in the imago state. Cold seems to have no ill effect on them. The eggs on twigs or trunks are not harmed even when covered by the ice of a sleet-storm. The caterpillars in the crevice of a wall, under dry leaves, in the chinks of the bark, or spun up in a leaf are not killed by cold many degrees below zero. The pupæ in the ground are not hurt though the earth freeze hard to the depth of several feet below their cells, and the pupæ in cocoons or among fallen leaves are equally unharmed by cold.

Frail as the moth imago seems, it can bear much injury without apparent discomfort, certainly without any sign of pain. In flying about, moths often break large pieces from their wings, but the loss of more than half of each wing does not seem to harm them at all. As long as enough wing is left to enable them to fly, they seem comfortable and can live unless chased by birds or bats. In this case the lack of speed caused by the lessened wing-power may prove fatal.

The loss of the antennæ is the greatest loss that can befall a moth except loss of life. Without antennæ the moth has no guide to its food-flowers, its mate, or the proper tree or plant on which to lay its eggs. It seems to have lost its connection with the world and is very helpless. Legs are essential for clinging to a support when at rest, but five of the six may be lost without making the moth helpless, for we have seen a sphingid moth, whose legs on one side had been broken off in some way, cling by the fore leg of the other side

5

and the ovipositor, which she curled around a support. Probably the male would use his claspers in such case, unless he could still cling by one leg, which seems possible.   This we have not seen, however.

We have not attempted to give histories of the loopers, or geometrid caterpillars, or of many noctuids. They are less noticeable, unless, indeed, they occur in great numbers, and most of them are less beautiful and interesting to beginners, than the *Sphingidæ, Ceratocampidæ,* and *Saturniidæ.*

It is to species of these families that the rug-weavers of the East turned for suggestions of the beautiful colors and combinations of colors they used in their rugs before the cheap aniline dyes reached them.

PART II

LIFE-HISTORIES

OF FORTY-THREE SPECIES, WITH ILLUSTRA-
TIONS OF THE CATERPILLAR AND MOTH OF
EACH AND OF A FEW SPECIES DESCRIBED.
ALL OF THESE HAVE A WIDE RANGE IN THE
UNITED STATES.

VII

SPHINGIDÆ

BRANCH,	ARTHROP'ODA	(" jointed-footed ").
CLASS,	HEXAP'ODA	(" six-footed ": insects).
ORDER,	LEPIDOP'TERA	(" scaly-winged ").
SUBORDER,	HETEROC'ERA	(" other-horned," i.e., antennæ not knobbed at the tip, like butterflies).
FAMILY,	SPHING'IDÆ	(" sphinx-like ").

THE moths of this family are often mistaken for humming-birds, when poised before flowers into whose deep nectaries they have thrust their long, slender tongues. They are called "humming-bird moths," and still oftener "hawk-moths," because they fly so swiftly and strongly. Some species fly at night, some at dusk, others in hot sunshine at noonday. They have long, narrow fore wings, short hind wings, and long, tapering abdomens. Their antennæ are long and slender, not feather-like as are those of the large spinning-moths, and not clubbed at the tip like those of most butterflies. The antennæ of the males are ciliate, while those of the females are not; both are fusiform. They are rarely pectinate.

The caterpillars have short hairs, or *setæ*, when very young, but are smooth or granulated when full grown. Most species have a caudal horn at some stage

69

of their life, though some have the horn replaced by a tubercle in the later molts, and others show no sign of horn or tubercle. Most of these larvæ have seven oblique lines on each side of the body, though the number may vary from four to ten.

Some of the caterpillars burrow in the earth to pupate, others spin very slight cocoons between leaves on the ground. We find no record of any which spins a dense cocoon. Most of the very young caterpillars spin a thread of silk as they crawl, probably as a guide, and many drop from the tree by this thread when disturbed.

Hemaris diffinis.

HEMARIS DIFFINIS

SUBFAMILY, MACROGLOSSI'NÆ ("long tongues").
GENUS, HEMA'RIS ("bloody-nose").
SPECIES, DIFFI'NIS ("unlike").

Our first sight of this species was when a box of the young caterpillars arrived by mail from Missouri, with a few bare twigs which we could not identify. Fortunately, the name of the crawlers was on the box, and One of Us promptly ran out to a bush of *Lonicera tartarica*, Tatarian honeysuckle, and brought in small sprays of leaves, which the hungry caterpillars began eating with every appearance of satisfaction. Other twigs were put in water to be ready when the leaves were gone from these, and then we sat down to examine our new treasures comfortably.

They were a little over half an inch long, pale green on the dorsum, or back, darker green on the sides, and thickly sprinkled with white granules. Each had three longitudinal brown stripes on the venter, or under side, and the legs and props were almost white, barred with dark brown. On the first segment and projecting over the head was a transverse double row of yellow granules larger than those of the body. On the eleventh segment was a caudal horn, long, slender, granulated, bright yellow at the base and blue-black

71

at the tip.   The spiracles were deep blue-black, ringed with palest blue.   The anal shield had a yellow tip. There were no oblique lines on the sides such as many sphingid larvæ have.   The spiracles were very conspicuous.

They were very hungry creatures, and there were a good many of them, and before they were full fed they ate every leaf of the Tatarian honeysuckle, and began on a bush of *Symphoricarpos racemosus*, the snowberry-bush, which is almost always found in old gardens or by the front door of very old farm-houses. They were not delicate at all, nor were any of them stung, so we reared the whole boxful, though nearly half of them lost the slender blue-black tips of their caudal horns at some stage of their life.   They reached us in May, and on the 16th of June they stopped eating, emptied their intestines, and began hurrying around the tins, growing purplish on their backs and duller in color all over.   When they tired of crawling, or spinning-time had come, each spun a slight web, holding leaves together, or fastening them to the bottom of the tin.

On the 18th the pupæ cast the caterpillar-skin, and the next day they had become brown, with darker wing-cases.   They were about an inch long, or a trifle longer, and rather slender, with no raised tongue-case.

We put all the pupæ in a box with glass set in the lid, giving them chopped sphagnum for bedding, and devoted ourselves to crawlers who were feeding voraciously, as is the habit of caterpillars.   We did not think of their emerging soon, but after some years of work with crawlers one seems to acquire an instinct about them, and to feel when any change is about to take place. So it happened that the Other of Us was up at dawn looking at the *diffinis* box, and saw the first moth emerge. What a surprise it was, too! The *Hemaris* moths are often called the "clear-winged" moths because their wings are transparent, except near the body and a band on the edge; but this moth, and that which quickly followed it up the side of the box, had black wings when they developed enough to be seen clearly. Another and another emerged, and then two or three at once, but all had the dark wings. It was a puzzle. Every other point agreed with the descriptions of *diffinis*. It was a puzzle which we had to leave unsolved for the time, for there was much to do among our boxes, and leaves were to be brought in from the woods and fields.

It was afternoon before we had another look at the moths, and they were flying about the box in a most lively manner, as they are day-flying moths, feeding at flowers in the hottest sunshine. Then the problem was solved. They were normal specimens in every respect, for the motion of flying had removed all the dark scales from the parts of the wings which should be transparent, and only the shining membrane was to be seen there. Thus we learned one fact which no book had told us — that the wings of *H. diffinis* were scale-covered until flying rubbed off the scales in certain parts.

They were very pretty moths. The outer wing-borders were black, while those of the hind wings, next the body, were marked with red. The upper part of the head and thorax was olive-yellow, and the sides

were yellow, while the abdomen was like the thorax at
its base, where it joined the thorax, but black elsewhere except the last two segments, which were clear
yellow, as was the under side of the thorax.   The legs
were black.

The next day more emerged, and we killed a few
with scales and without, to photograph, but we could
not get one with all the scales on because the least
breath or touch detached them.   Still our photograph
gives an idea of the newly emerged moths as well as
of those which have flown.

Finding that the moths emerged so early in the season, we planned to have a second brood, so put several
in a cage, giving them flowers and drops of honey to
feed on.   There was no feeding, however, and finally
it occurred to One of Us that the moths usually fed in
the bright sunlight, so she moved the box into a sunny
place, leaving one end in shade to give coolness if desired.   In less than five minutes the moths were feeding, and in a short time two mated.

In four days the female *diffinis* laid two hundred
and eight eggs, then died.   The male had been set
free after mating.   Seven days later the first eggs
hatched, giving little caterpillars about an eighth of an
inch long, pale yellow in color, with a white collar, or
transverse raised band, on the first segment, and
short, colorless hairs, or setæ, all over.   The caudal
horn was yellow, then turned gray, then black.

These little caterpillars paid no attention to their
shells, but went to the leaves and began eating at
once.   They drank eagerly.   Three days later they
molted, coming out a quarter of an inch long, green

Hemaris diffinis.

above, almost purple beneath, with a crest of yellow on the first segment. The caudal horn was long, rough, blue-black, with yellow on the sides of its base. The legs, props, and spiracles were blue-black. The head was round and yellow, with pink mouth-parts.

Three days later they molted again, much as before, but the head was greener, no hairs were to be seen, and the substigmatal ridge was yellower. This is the ridge below the spiracles, or *stigmata*. Three days later they molted for the third time, and were decidedly larger. Nine of them changed to a soft chocolate-brown color, with a golden crest on the first segment, and yellow at the base of the blue-black horn. The others were pale green on the dorsum, yellow-green on the sides, and brown on the venter, with longitudinal darker brown stripes, and had no ridge. Two, which molted later, had black heads, light brown backs, and dark brown sides and venters; and one was golden-yellow on the dorsum and brown elsewhere. All were granulated with yellow-white, and all had blue-black horns with yellow at the base.

The fourth molt was four days later, and most of the caterpillars were colored as before, except that their legs and props were light, barred with brownish black, and the spiracles were blue-black, with a white dot at top and bottom, and a white circle around each spiracle. The spiracles looked like the port-holes of an ocean steamer. One brown caterpillar came out with the head almost black and the body deep brown granulated with white, except the first and last segments, which were bright orange with orange granules. The legs, props, and venter were deep brown.

Six days later the first ones turned purplish on the dorsum, and prepared to spin. They were from an inch and three quarters to two inches long. The next day they spun, and four days later they pupated, having passed from egg to pupa in twenty-four days.

The pupæ were slender, the wing-covers being darker brown than the body. The tongue-case was not raised.

To feed this last brood we had to forage in our neighbor's garden and beg for snowberry-twigs, for our bush was entirely stripped; but neighbors are very kind when we need help of this sort, and we had the satisfaction of carrying the family through two generations, and starting a third through eggs from the moths which emerged the next spring. These eggs we gave away, however, being content with two generations and wishing to give the snowberry- and honeysuckle-bushes time to recover from their defoliation. It is not often that we have to strip a bush or tree so completely, but it did no harm as far as we could learn.

Mr. Beutenmüller gives the range of *diffinis* as "from Canada to Florida, and westward to Missouri and Iowa." The only place where we have seen the moths flying in numbers is Wonalancet, among the White Mountains, where we saw scores of them feeding at the large pasture-thistles, and so overcome by the fragrance or the nectar that they were easily caught with a small box and its cover, sometimes two or three being shut in at one scoop. They flew at midday and looked like large and beautiful bees as they hovered over the thistles, thrusting their long tongues far down into the purple-pink flower-heads, and not giving up their places to real bees, butterflies, beetles, or even the swiftly darting humming-birds which came flashing in among the thistles' visitors, startling the butterflies and sending the bees humming away to other thistles. In our experience there is no place like an old hillside pasture in August with a good growth of pasture-thistles for giving great variety of insects and for good views of humming-birds.

Until very lately the spring brood of *H. diffinis* was thought to be a different species and was called *H. tenuis*, but Mr. Ellison A. Smyth, Jr., has proved that the two are the same species by rearing *diffinis* in July from eggs of *tenuis* laid in May, and rearing *tenuis* from eggs of *diffinis*.

Hemaris thysbe, next of kin to *H. diffinis*, was also found feeding at the thistles, and was caught in the same easy way.

VIII

SUBFAMILY CHŒROCAMPINÆ

THIS subfamily (the "hog-caterpillars") is named from a fancied resemblance of the caterpillars to pigs.

Many of the species have the third and fourth segments larger than the others, and some draw the head and first segment into the second, telescope fashion, when at rest and when frightened.

The moths have large, prominent heads, and fly very swiftly. They are very strong, and have a habit of darting downward when startled; so the net should always be placed beneath them and swung upward to catch them.

Amphion nessus.

AMPHION NESSUS

GENUS, AMPHI'ON (a son of Zeus).
SPECIES, NES'SUS (one of the centaurs).

We found on the under side of woodbine-leaves
some sphingid eggs with a luster like mother-of-pearl,
and having colors more or less iridescent. Through
the shell we could see the yellowish larva lying curled
up, so we knew that the eggs would hatch very soon.

The next day the pale yellow caterpillars ate their
way out, and began to eat and drink — or rather to
drink and then to eat — at once. Their heads were
large and flat, and had a fold of yellower skin just
behind them, not a crest on the first segment, but a
fold of skin. The caudal horn was long, slender,
straight, and ended in a square-cut tip with a seta at
each end. These setæ projected almost horizontally
on each side of the horn, giving it a branched look.
The fourth segment was slightly swollen.

The caterpillars ate holes through the leaves and
grew a little greener after eating.

Six days later they molted, coming out three times
as long as when they hatched, a great increase of size
for the first molt. The head was blue-green, with
faint white face-lines, flat, and held almost horizontal.
The legs and props were blue-green like the body,

79

which was unmarked.   The caudal horn was brown at
base, black above, and very rough with white setæ, and
was held bent backward in a line with the dorsum.

Seven days later the second molt took place.   The
head was blue-green, with faint white face-lines.   The
body was blue-green, with transverse lines of white
granules, white subdorsal lines, and a dark green dorsal line.   There was a faint suggestion of white obliques.
The legs and props were green.   The horn was brownish white at base, black above, and rough with white
setæ.

In this molt some larvæ had pink horns, paler behind.   All the caudal horns were shorter than before.

The third molt followed in four days.   The head
was very round, granulated with darker green on the
sides, but with no granules between the yellow-white,
opaque face-lines.

The body was green, with yellow-white granules.
The subdorsal lines were yellow-white, edged above
with darker green, and the dorsal line was of the same
darker green.   The obliques were yellow, edged with
green above.   On the thoracic segments were faint
indications of lateral and stigmatal lines of yellow-
white.   The swelling of the fourth segment was more
marked, and the third segment was slightly larger than
the first or second.   The anal shield was edged with
yellow-white.   The legs and anal props were green;
the abdominal props green, with a pink band above
the plantæ.   The horn was short, stout, triangular,
red above and pink behind, with a deep red line from
the end of the dorsal line to the tip of the horn.

In this stage several of the larvæ came out brown

instead of green, and one was of a clear wine-color, with the obliques and other body-lines of pink edged above with deep claret-color. The granules and face-lines were pale yellow. Some larvæ had ten obliques. Some had no pink on the abdominal props.

All were more sluggish in this stage and the next than any other larvæ we have reared, and were most easily detached from the vine, the slightest jar suffi-cing to send them to the ground. If removed from a twig and laid on their backs, they did not even turn over until they were hungry and had to crawl to a leaf to feed.

The fourth molt followed four days later. All came out pale brown granulated with yellow, each granule having a black dot in its center. The head was bi-lobed, dark brown between the yellow face-lines, rough with black and a few pale yellow granules. Outside of the face-lines the granules were yellow. The body was dotted with black. On the thoracic segments were black dorsal, subdorsal, lateral, and stigmatal lines, the dorsal line being represented on the abdominal segments by a black patch at the juncture of every two segments. The obliques were distinct and almost black — nine in most instances, ten in a few. The horn was very short, stout, and rough. The spiracles were black, with a yellow dot at each end, and encircled by a yellow line. The legs and props were brown, the anal props being darker than the others, and the anal shield was of this darker brown, with a dorsal line ex-tending to its tip and a yellow edge. The third and fourth segments were slightly swollen — just enough to be out of focus in the photograph.

In this stage the larvæ twitched from side to side when disturbed, but were otherwise very sluggish.

Ten days later the granules had disappeared and all the marks had grown paler. Then the caterpillars looked grayish and dusty on the dorsum, and stopped eating. They were three inches long, a few being shorter.

Some spun a few threads fastening leaves to the tin; others merely lay on the bottom of the tin, and pupated three days later.

The pupæ were an inch and a half long, very dark brown, and coffee-colored between the abdominal segments, which were pitted. The wing-covers were rough. There was a slightly pointed tubercle at the base of each antenna. The anal hook was long, slender, and bifid at the tip.

Out of doors these caterpillars are easy prey for parasitic flies, and among their most common enemies is *Apanteles congregatus*, whose yellow cocoons form a sort of crust over the body of the caterpillar.

The moths are found "from Canada to Florida, and westward to Iowa," according to Mr. Beutenmüller. They fly by day as well as in the evening. They are common in eastern Massachusetts and western Vermont, but Mr. Beutenmüller finds them not common near New York.

We have found the eggs in May and June, and larvæ from June till October, showing that eggs must be laid later than June.

The food-plants given are grape, woodbine, and *Epilobium;* but we have not chanced to find larvæ or eggs on the last.

The moths are in shades of rich brown and yellow, the abdomen being of deep, velvety brown, with a band of canary-yellow between the fourth and fifth segments, and white tufts on the under side. The wings are somewhat "cut out," but not enough to call them notched. The antennæ are simple in the female, ciliate on the under side in the male, and hooked at the end. The tongue is about an inch long.

The moths feed at phlox, sweet-william, verbenas, and such flowers, and lay their eggs at dusk.

THYREUS ABBOTII

GENUS, THY'REUS (a large shield, the tubercle of the larva).
SPECIES, ABBOT'II (Abbot's).

This is one of the most common sphingid caterpillars, feeding on grape and woodbine, and we had had many half-grown specimens which we reared successfully before we had eggs to give us the life-history. We knew a woodbine on which we had often found these crawlers and *Deidamia inscripta*, and to this we went for eggs of both. On June 8 we found plenty of *inscripta* eggs and a few which might be *abbotii* or *myron*. We marked several sprays of vine having no eggs on them, and went the next day to examine them. It was probable that we should find eggs, because a moth usually oviposits for several successive nights in the same neighborhood, and this woodbine covered a long wall, giving ample room for many larvæ to feed in comfort. It was therefore not a surprise to find several eggs on the marked sprays, and we boxed them with the satisfaction of having the exact date of their laying. The eggs were bright apple-green, almost globular, and finely shagreened, as seen under a lens. They were on the upper side of the leaves, each on a spray by itself, except one egg which was on a tendril just over a leaf. In seven days they hatched.

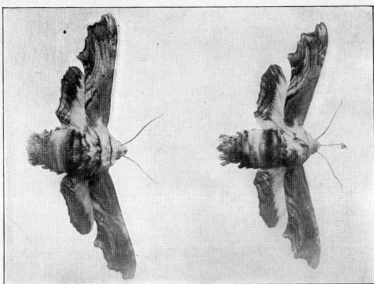

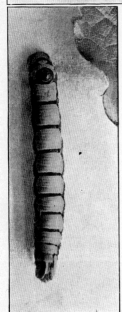

The caterpillars were very small and pale pinkish green, with slender, dark caudal horns. They ate a little of their egg-shells, but ate nothing else until the third day, when they began to eat holes in woodbine-leaves. They grew glassy green after eating.

Six days later they molted and came out very different, being covered with a white "bloom" which concealed the pale green color almost entirely. The legs and props were green, and the horn was like a slender shaft set on a mound, the mound being yellow, with a black patch in front, and the shaft white. The crawlers ate their cast skins and were very easily disturbed, twitching and jerking their bodies violently when the leaves were touched.

In three days the second molt took place, the only changes being increased size, the dark color which made the spiracles noticeable, and the loss of the caudal horn. In its place was the yellow mound, with a black semicircle around the base in front.

Five days later they molted for the third time, and changed even more than before. Part had the head brown, of a pale "ashes-of-roses" shade, with wide dark brown bands from the mouth-parts over the face and head. These bands continued over the thoracic segments, diminishing in size after the first segment. The body was of ashes-of-roses lined with darker brown, and looked like snake-skin, especially when examined with a lens. The dorsal line was dark; the dorsum darker than the sides, with a wavy, light subdorsal line. The venter and legs were pink-brown. The props were ashes-of-roses banded with dark brown, except the anal props, which were marked like snake-skin, as was the anal shield. In place of the caudal "mound" was a very large, round tubercle of three shades of brown with a black center, giving the effect of a bright eye.

The other caterpillars were strikingly different. They had bright leaf-green patches on the head, one large green patch on the dorsum of each segment, one on the substigmatal region of each segment, and three or four on the pink-brown venter. These patches were marked off by browns of the same shades as those of the other form of coloring, and the caudal tubercles were alike in both forms. The anal shield and props of the green form had patches of green.

The caterpillars fed for five days, growing large very rapidly; then the green ones grew dingy and stopped eating, and the brown ones grew lead-colored on the dorsum; and both kinds curled up in horse-shoe shape, grew moist, and pupated six days later, with no fourth molt. Probably this omission of a molt was due to the intense heat, for several species of caterpillars feeding at this time molted but three times before pupating.

The caterpillars were very excitable and reared the anal end in the air, brandishing it and vibrating it like a snake's head, which it really resembled enough to frighten birds. We have seen orioles try to pick up an *abbotii* larva on our woodbine, and dart away with a scream when it lifted its snake-like anal end with the tubercle shining like an eye. The caterpillars make a squeaking noise; how they make it we do not know.

The pupæ were an inch and an eighth long, not

stout or slender, dark brown, smooth, with no raised tongue-case.   Out of doors they are formed underground.

Usually *abbotii* has passed through four molts before pupation, in our experience, and has had a larval life of at least four weeks instead of but twenty-five days.

The moth flies just before and just after sunset.   Its head and thorax are chocolate-brown, with a blue-gray sheen sometimes; the abdomen is blackish next the body, then brown, then dark again at the tip, which is tufted.   The fore wings are notched, dark brown at base, lighter till close to the margin, with dark streaks and lines.   The hind wings are bright canary-yellow with brownish borders.

The male's antennæ are ciliate, turned back at the tip, while those of the female are simple.

It is very easy to watch a moth lay her eggs and collect them as she leaves them, for she lays one on a leaf, not always on the upper side, then flies about until the next egg must be laid, and deposits it at a distance of several feet from that last laid.   This might be interpreted as a " wise maternal instinct" which allowed each of the future young plenty of food-space, but for the fact that the mother soon flutters back and lays an egg not far from the one she has just laid, and continues ovipositing in the same neighborhood, and though each egg is laid at a distance of several feet from the last one, several eggs may be gathered in a square yard.   This would indicate a short memory or lack of observation of direction and locality — or a want of that " wise maternal instinct" so much lauded by sentimentalists.   However this may be, the moth is interesting as well as the caterpillar.

Orioles, robins, and gray squirrels eat the caterpillars greedily, though occasionally frightened by the snake-like anal end.

Parasitic flies, especially *microgaster*, destroy many of the half-grown larvæ.

DEIDAMIA INSCRIPTA

GENUS,   DEIDA'MIA.
SPECIES,   INSCRIP'TA ("marked").

One of Us sat on some steps one day watching a gray squirrel descending the Japanese woodbine on the side of the house. He had reached an ornamental ledge on which English sparrows had built a ragged nest of straws and feathers, and he had given a vigorous kick with one hind leg and another with the other hind leg, scattering all the straws and feathers to the winds, and was quietly continuing his descent as if nothing had interrupted it and his only object was the nut in the hand of One of Us, when a slight movement of a leaf caught the attention of both. One of Us saw a smooth green head at the edge of the leaf moving in a way which suggested a caterpillar eating. What the squirrel saw she does not know, but he hastened his steps. Luckily One of Us was nearer the leaf than he was, and had leaf and caterpillar in her hands before Bunny arrived. Bunny's mother had caught an *abbotii* caterpillar just as One of Us was about to take it, and had deliberately sat up and eaten the squirming thing as a boy sometimes eats a pickled cucumber bought at the corner grocery at recess; so One of Us had learned from practical experience that squirrels were caterpillar-hunters and that it was well to be first in the field.

The caterpillar saved from sudden death proved very nearly full grown, and was different from any One of Us had seen. This was exciting, and she searched the vine as far up as she could see, and on the two sides of the house, but found no more caterpillars like this one which was eating peacefully in her pocket tin. The next step was to find out what it was, and she looked through all the descriptions of sphingid cater-pillars, and at all the pictures of them she could find; but none was just like it, so she fed the crawler, hoping to identify the moth it would make. This was a vain hope. The caterpillar pupated finely, but a few weeks later was found to be only a pupa-skin filled with fungus.

This was one of the many blows which fall upon the caterpillar-hunter or entomologist, and must be expected.

The next June One of Us was searching a woodbine, the common American woodbine, and found on one lobe of a leaf six pale green eggs, and on another seven more. Some of the eggs had been laid longer than others, for they had turned yellowish. Probably they were laid by different moths. All had the shells marked like honeycomb or hammered silver, and the oldest ones showed the little larvæ through the transparent shells. One of Us searched farther and found an egg on a tendril, just where it curled at one tip, and then she spied an egg set among a cluster of flower-buds, and of exactly their size, shape, and color at that stage of their growth. After this she examined many clusters of buds and found many more eggs; then, on the very young leaves, came upon some tiny caterpillars with caudal horns. These had a reddish patch just behind the base of the caudal horn, and this is not usual in sphingid caterpillars. Most of those we have reared have had no distinguishing marks when first hatched, but have been plain green or yellowish caterpillars with caudal horns.

She put eggs into one tin and larvæ and a leaf or two into a larger one, and carried them home.

The eggs began hatching at one o'clock in the afternoon, and the little caterpillars were almost a quarter of an inch long, yellow-green, with the caudal horns yellow and covered densely with black setæ, and had a white bristle at the tip of each. Just behind the horn was a reddish patch.

The empty shells were iridescent, and each caterpillar ate nearly all the shell from which it came. They did not drink water as eagerly as most young caterpillars, nor did they grow as green after eating, though they ate for six days before molting.

After this first molt they were less than half an inch long, yellow-green, with a yellow subdorsal line from head to horn, a green dorsal line, and a yellow transverse line — like a thick fold of skin — between each two abdominal segments. As usual with sphingid larvæ in the first two stages, they had short setæ all over. The head was yellow-green and bilobed, and the feet and props were yellow-green also. The horn was long, slender, and rough with black setæ, except at the tip, which was white with white setæ. The reddish spot remained behind the caudal horn. The anal plate and props had a glassy look. The fourth segment was slightly swollen.

Three days later they were yellow-green dotted with yellow, with a yellow subdorsal line, and a yellow, wavy stigmatal line on the first three segments, also seven yellow oblique lines edged above with dark green. The head showed very faint yellow face-lines, and the legs and props were yellower than the body.

In this stage they had a funny way of resting with all the props holding a midrib or stem, while the fore part of the body was thrown up and backward until the head was over the ninth segment, mouth-parts and legs being up in the air. They still liked rather young leaves, though not the very youngest ones as in the last stage.

Four days later they molted, and this time there was a decided change in their appearance. They were seven eighths of an inch long, and the head was apple-green, with yellow face-lines, and was rough.

The body was of a bluer green than the head, and the third and fourth segments were slightly swollen; there was a yellow stigmatal line on the first three segments — the thoracic segments — and also a yellow subdorsal line edged above with dark green. The dorsal line was dark green, and the body had transverse rows of yellow dots, except the first segment. This time there were eight yellow obliques edged above with dark green. Seven is the normal number of oblique lines for sphingid larvæ. The legs were yellow, the props green. The caudal horn was long, slender, green at base, black above, white at tip, and

Deidamia inscripta.

rough with black granules. It was depressed or bent backward till nearly horizontal.

The third molt followed in four days, and then the caterpillars were an inch and a quarter long, with the third and fourth segments slightly thickened. The head was bright green, with two bright yellow face-lines, continued as subdorsals over the bright green body. The venter was bluer green than the rest of the body, and not dotted. The body had yellow transverse lines instead of dots, the lines being broken in the stigmatal region. The horn was short, almost triangular, greenish at base, rough with brown granules in the middle, and yellow at tip and on the sides, up which extended the seventh pair of obliques. The anal plate was edged with yellow. The spiracles were conspicuous for the first time, being white with a blue-black crescent on each side. The other lines were the same as before.

The caterpillars ate and grew for five days, and then surprised us by turning pink on the dorsum, losing their grasp of the stems, and stopping eating. All this meant approaching pupation; but they had not molted the regulation "four times," though they were about two and a quarter inches in length.

On looking over three years' records of each box we found several variations. Some had but seven obliques, while the rest had eight on each side. Some had no yellow dots below the stigmatal line, while others were dotted almost to the ventral line. Some caudal horns were marked up the front and down the back with a continuation of the dark dorsal line; some had no green at base, and two were wholly yellow; a few were pink

and yellow.   One boxful molted but three times, omit-
ting the second molt, and fed for twenty days; another
lot molted four times and fed for sixteen days, while
one molted four times and fed for twenty-six days.
In most cases the obliques almost disappeared before
pupation.

These caterpillars grew very sluggish after the last
molt, and when they stopped eating crawled very
slowly about the tin, then stayed still and pupated
without spinning.

In the stage before the last molt they were very
petulant when disturbed, twitching their bodies and
jerking from side to side like the caterpillars of *abbotii*.

The swollen segments seem to show their kinship
with *Amphi'on nes'sus, Ampeloph'aga my'ron* and *A.
chœ'rilus, Philam'pelus pando'rus* and *P. a'chemon,* all
common on woodbine, and most of them on grape.

The pupæ were a little over an inch in length,
brown speckled with darker brown, the dorsum and
wing-covers being much darker.   They had a sharp
cremaster, a pointed projection on top of the head, and
one on each eye-cover.   Under a lens the dark speckles showed as pits.   The pupæ were slender and not
as active as many sphingid pupæ, hardly writhing
when held in the hand.

The fore wings of the moth are in shades of brown,
gray, and silver-gray, with a white discal dot.   The
hind wings are of deep rust-red, with lines of brown
and gray, and gray borders.   The body is gray, and
the abdomen has brown spots on the dorsum and tip.
The whole under surface is much lighter than the
upper.

DEILEPHILA LINEATA

GENUS,   DEILE'PHILA   ("evening lover").
SPECIES,   LINEA'TA   ("lined").

"Here's a bug for you.   Take it quick; I'm afraid it will die!   I shut it up tight in this box to keep it safe, and it may smother, though I came as fast as I could," said "the old doctor" one morning.   Of course we knew that there was no danger of smothering the caterpillar, but we were eager to see what kind could have induced the doctor to box it, for he was one of those unfortunate persons who shiver and "feel creepy" at sight of any crawling thing, and we fully appreciated his kindness in overcoming his feeling so far as to bring the creature even in a closed box.   We opened the box, and a very lively caterpillar crawled quickly over the edge, while the doctor jumped back, and the family cried, "What a monster!"   It was three and a half inches long and as large as most third fingers of medium-sized persons.   It was bright green, with orange spots on each side, and a caudal horn.

We asked where it was found.

"In my melon-patch, on the ground," replied the doctor.

"Has the melon-patch any purslane in it?" asked

the Other of Us, with a twinkle, for the doctor prided himself on his garden.

"John was just weeding it out when we found the bug. Why?" said the doctor.

"Because this kind of caterpillar feeds on 'pusley' in preference to other things, though it will eat turnip, buckwheat, watermelon, dock, chickweed, apple, plum, currant, grape, woodbine, gooseberry, and evening primrose," said One of Us; and after expostulating with the doctor for calling a fine caterpillar a "bug," we went to find "pusley," or purslane, for it and to put it away.

The next June we were fortunate enough to get a fine batch of eggs of this *Deile'phila linea'ta,* or "white-lined morning sphinx," so called from the light lines on the wings of the moth. The eggs were small in proportion to the size of the moth, ovoid, and yellow-green, growing bluer. Like all sphingid eggs, they became depressed on one side after a day or two. They hatched in six days.

The little caterpillars were not quite a quarter of an inch long, pale green, with short, smooth caudal horns which turned gray at the tip. The head was round and held almost horizontal instead of nearly vertical, and was covered with gray setæ. The setæ on the body were dark enough to be noticed without a lens. When disturbed the little crawlers dropped by a silken thread as spiders do. They did not eat their shells at all, and were very active, crawling about the purslane stems much of the time. Part of them were given woodbine, since it was easier to get. On the second day some of them showed a distinct brownish-red

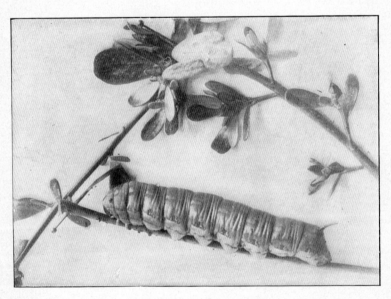

Deilephila lineata (small specimens).

dorsal line from the now black horn half-way to the head, giving a pinkish appearance to that part of the body. A few had the first five or six segments notice-ably pinkish, and all looked black-striped from the rows of black setæ — without a lens. With a glass the setæ showed clearly. Next day their heads were the color of old ivory, and their bodies had almost as glassy an appearance as those of young *T. abbot'ii* larvæ.

The first molt came on the eighth day and changed the caterpillars somewhat, besides the increased length. Their heads were smooth, orange-brown, and bilobed. Their bodies were dark green speckled with lighter green. On the dorsum of the first segment was a divided horny plate of lighter green. A faint yellow stigmatal line showed on the first three seg-ments, and there was a bright yellow subdorsal line. The legs and props were lighter green, and the horn was light green at base, black and rough above. Some had no yellow lines. In some the anal shield was orange-brown.

In four days they molted again, being now half an inch long, with no setæ. The orange-brown head was speckled with a lighter shade. The body was almost black, rather faintly speckled with yellow-white. A bright yellow subdorsal line extended from head to horn, and on it, on each segment, was a yellow patch. There was a stigmatal wavy line of bright yellow. The spiracles showed yellow-white. The horn was orange-brown at base, black and rough above. The body tapered from the third segment to the head. In this stage they ate woodbine much better than grape,

7

which was also given them, and as purslane was not easy to get, all were given woodbine, and throve on it.

The third molt took place five days later. This time the body was black, with transverse lines of white dots, and velvety black on the dorsum and between the segments there. The marks and lines were as before. The legs and props were orange-brown, and the horn was shining black, rough, and ended in two setæ. The anal shield was black, speckled and edged with yellow-white, and looked placed very high above the props, instead of ending low down between them.

Four days later they molted for the fourth time, being then an inch and a half long, with small heads, and pale-green bodies with transverse black lines from the stigmatal line to the dorsal band of velvety black. Between each two segments this band gave off a short branch. On this short black band was placed the yellow patch. The subdorsal and stigmatal lines were bright yellow. The dorsal plate on the first segment was orange-brown speckled with lighter brown, as were the anal plate and props. The legs and props were orange-brown, the spiracles yellow-white encircled with black. The venter was paler green and mottled, as well as striated, with black.

The caterpillars varied even more in this stage, some having the head, dorsal plate, and the anal props and shield green speckled with orange, the body hardly striated with black, and on each segment a black bar with an orange spot set in it. The dorsal black band was faint and divided lengthwise by a green line. The bodies tapered from the third segment to the head.

All the caterpillars had a queer way of moving the caudal horn as a finger is moved up and down without bending it or moving the hand. They were very active, and dropped from the stems when disturbed, instead of clinging faster as most caterpillars do. They jerked the fore part of the body from side to side, as *T. abbotii* larvæ do when startled.

Four days later they molted for the fifth time, and there came out two distinct forms of coloration. One was mustard-yellow striated with blue-black, with a yellow dot on each segment, and yellow lines as before, but with the horn longer in proportion and still rough, and the spiracles orange encircled with black. The other form was apple-green with much less black, the subdorsal line being a series of yellow spots inclosing an orange dot, and set on the black patch on each segment, with a very faint trace of yellow connecting the spots. One caterpillar had no orange. They moved their horns like fingers or antennæ in this stage also.

For six days they fed voraciously, keeping us busy enough in supplying leaves, and they grew very fast, the shortest being over three inches long, the longest nearly three and a half.

After each molt every caterpillar ate up his cast skin even to the rough horn, leaving only the mask. This habit of eating the cast skin certainly removes one trace of caterpillar presence, but it seems very useless, if this is the cause, for the great oblong " balls " of excrement are a conspicuous guide by which one can track a caterpillar all over the garden — if it crawls as far as that. Caterpillars digest their food so rapidly that excretion must be very frequent.

After once knowing *lineata* in all its stages we have often found nearly full-grown larvæ on the unshaded ground in the garden, feeding on purslane, with the midday sun beating down on them. This is unusual, for most moth-larvæ, even if feeding at noon, would be under the shelter of leaves or behind a tree-trunk out of the direct rays of the sun. We have never found *lineata* on woodbine, but other entomologists have.

On the thirtieth day from the egg they began to crawl restlessly about, stopped eating, chewed holes in the scrim over the box, and then spun loose webs like a fish-net between leaves and the tin, crawling about for nearly two days before spinning. In three days the pupæ were free from the caterpillar-skin. Imagine our surprise a few years later to have a brood curl up quietly without spinning a thread, and part of another brood go into earth only deep enough to cover them, and there pupate without spinning. This shows that one brood does not teach everything about the habits of the crawlers.

The pupæ were nearly two inches long, slender, slightly pitted on the abdomen and of a pale tan-color — the lightest-colored sphingid pupa we know, except *Ampelophaga myron*. The head was much prolonged, the tongue-case not raised above the wing-covers. The eyes were well defined. The anal hook, or cremaster, ended in two short points.

The eggs of the brood so fully described were laid on June 10, and on August 11 the first moth emerged between 12:45 and 2 P.M., while we were at luncheon.

The moths are very beautiful. The head, thorax, and

top of the abdomen are olive-brown, the patagia being
edged with white, and the abdomen having a dorsal
line of white edged with black broken on the basal
segments. The fore wings are olive-brown, crossed by
a band of buff, the inner end of which is cyanic white.
The hind wings are smoky brown at the base and
outer edge, with a broad bright pink band across the
middle. The sides of the abdomen have a pink band
that does not extend all the way to the tip, and alter-
nate black and white patches. The wing-fringes are
white. The under side of the wings is grayer, with a
fainter buff band across both, a little pink being sometimes present on the hind wings. The wings are
speckled more or less with almost black, and have
some irregular patches of the same color. Along the
costa of the fore wings, for nearly half its length, lies
a line of very long, hair-like scales. The under side of
the abdomen is paler than the upper, and the under
side of the palpi is white. The antennæ are redder
brown, with white near the recurved tip. The tongue
is over an inch long. The eyes are large and prominent, the legs colored like the under side of the abdomen.

The moths fly from early morning till after dark,
perhaps all night. We have taken them feeding at
verbenas, honeysuckle, phlox, and the yellow day-
lilies. Into the last they dive so far that they can be
caught by closing the petals over them. We have
found them laying eggs on purslane at dusk.

PHILAMPELUS PANDORUS AND ACHEMON

GENUS,   PHILAM'PELUS ("vine-lover").

SPECIES   { PANDO'RUS
          { A'CHEMON   (Greek proper name).

We had had so many caterpillars of these two species, both large and small, with horns and without, that it was somewhat startling to discover that we had not their life-histories.   It was mortifying too, for we might have had them many times over when the moths emerged, and the only way to regain self-respect was to get them.   One of Us knew a woodbine sprawling in long trails over a mass of cobblestones left on a hilltop by a retreating glacier, and this woodbine had furnished crawlers of both kinds for several summers. There was, then, good hope of finding eggs of both species if she hit upon just the right time.   The weather was intensely hot, the sky cloudless, the hilltop unshaded, so One of Us arose with the robins, the earliest birds in that part of the country, and walked up the hill between four and five o'clock in the morning, much distracted by the songs and glimpses of birds she wished to follow and watch, and much tempted by rudbeckias and meadow-rue in the fields by the way.   The cobblestones were hard to the knees, but stooping was too back-breaking, so she knelt

Philampelus pandorus.

among the vines, examining every lobe of every leaf
of every long trail of vine, and finding many eggs and
a few hatchlings. The eggs were laid singly on the
upper side of nearly full-grown leaves, except in two
instances, when each egg was laid on a grass-blade
which lay across a leaf and an inch and a half or two
inches above it. It was hot work kneeling in the sun
and grew hotter every moment, and the passing farmers
nearly tumbled off their wagons in their efforts to see
what "the Bug-woman" could be doing, while the
boys who were driving cows to the pastures over the hill
and down the other side made a pretense of picking
up stones to throw at laggards, or cutting unnecessary switches from the one small willow, in the hope
of making out why One of Us was on her knees in
that place at that hour.

After careful examination several long sprays were
marked as having no eggs on them, and One of Us
went home, hot but triumphant, to repeat the performance several times, getting eggs each time and
learning the exact date of the laying of the eggs found
on the marked sprays. Then came the waiting to
find out if she had both species or only one, and this
was patience-trying.

The eggs were almost globular, dark, bright green,
and grew yellower before hatching. The egg-period
was six days for some, and seven for others found in
cooler weather.

The young crawlers had large, round, pale-green
heads, yellow-green bodies, feet, and props, and dark
caudal horns exactly as long as their bodies between
horn and head, and ending in two setæ. Around the

base of the horn and extending a little way down the
anal shield was a red-brown patch, very noticeable in
every case but one, and plain to see in that one. The
caterpillars ate their egg-shells to the leaf in most
instances, then crawled quickly up the midrib on the
under side of a fresh leaf, drank from the drops sprinkled on it, and soon began eating holes through the
parenchyma. The two species were alike so far, and
we did not know whether we had both or not. They
ate woodbine very well, and were satisfactory, never
meddling with each other or hurting each other acci-
dentally.

In four days they molted for the first time, and still
were alike, so much alike that no scrutiny with a
fifteen-diameters lens could detect any difference.
Their heads were small, round, flat, green, and held
nearly horizontal, giving them a crouching look as if
flattened along the leaf. Their bodies were green,
finely dotted with yellow-white, and having pale yellow-white subdorsal lines from head to horn. The
third segment was slightly swollen. The legs and
props were green, and the horn was as long as the
body, slender, almost black, rough, and red-brown
at base and on the anal shield. This color varied
from red-brown to wine-color. At the base of the
horn in front, on the red color, was a dark red dot
almost black, and evidently the center of the tubercle
which would replace the horn in some future molt.
The caterpillars still ate holes through the leaves.

Three days later they molted again. This time the
two kinds could be distinguished and separated.

Pandorus had the head small, flat, and held horizon-

Philampelus achemon.

tal, as before, and head and first segment were of a bright, clear yellow-green. The second and third segments were speckled with black, and the whole body was bright green, with a dark dorsal line, very faint yellow subdorsal lines, and five oblique, regular oval patches — not lines — encircled with black and surrounding the unnoticeable spiracles. These obliques were the unmistakable characteristic of *pandorus*. The legs and props were green, and the horn was long, very slender, deep red with black setæ all over, yellow at base with a black spot in front, and curled forward over the back. The third segment was more swollen than before.

Achemon had the head flat, small, clear green, and held horizontal. The body was clear, bright green, dotted with yellow, and had no black dots. The yellow subdorsals were clearer than those of *pandorus*. There were six pairs of obliques of yellow edged above with dark green, longer and narrower than those of *pandorus*, as well as one pair more in number. The legs and props were green, the anal plate was edged with yellow, and the horn was long, very slender, deep red, and almost black at tip, its base being yellow in front with a shining black dot, and red behind, the color extending part-way down the anal shield. Instead of curling forward, like the horn of *pandorus*, *achemon's* horn was held perpendicular or bent backward until it made a line with the dorsum. The third segment was more swollen.

Both species now ate through the leaf at the margin, beginning at the tip of a lobe, and working down. After every molt they ate the cast skins, except the masks.

Pandorus molted three days later, some coming out green as before, with the second and third segments dotted with white encircled by black, the other segments having these ringed dots on the sublateral and stigmatal regions only, and losing them in a day or two. The obliques had now the salmon tint of those of the full-fed larva, and the horn was short in proportion to the size of the body, and had at base in front a yellow tubercle with a black circle about it and a shining black central dot. The third segment was very large, and the fourth decidedly larger than the other abdominal segments, though not as large as the third. The caterpillar could draw the head and first two segments completely within the third. Other larvæ were brown of various shades, marked like the green ones.

Achemon also molted in three days, and showed the same variety of brown and green coloring. The head was plain green, or brown, round, and no longer flat. The body was green, or brown, the first segment dotted with white; the second and third segments were covered thickly with white dots ringed with black, and the other segments had similar black-ringed white dots below the lateral line, and white dots above it. The legs and props were green, or brown. The horn was bright, deep red, almost black at the tip, shorter in proportion to the body, and having at the base in front a bright yellow tubercle with a black circle and central dot. The obliques were long, narrow, broken white ovals, with a black line around each.

Three days later *pandorus* molted for the fourth time. Some were green, some greenish brown, some

Philampelus achemon.

pinkish brown, some clear fawn-color, others chocolate-brown, and one was almost black, growing purple-brown as it grew larger, as if the color were diluted to cover the increased surface. Each had a dark dorsal line, lighter broken subdorsal lines, the first five segments speckled with black, the sixth to tenth segments having two black dots each on the dorsum and a few on the venter; all were lighter in color on the dorsum and dark on the venter; the obliques and tubercles were as before, and the horn had disappeared with the cast skin. The legs and props were of the body-color, whatever that was. The darker larvæ had obliques almost white instead of salmon-color. The spiracles were dark. No caterpillar had more than five obliques on a side, and one had but four, the fifth being merely suggested.

The fourth molt of *achemon* was four days after the third. The caterpillars came out green, greenish brown, pinkish brown, and chocolate-brown, but none was as dark as the darkest *pandorus*. The head was plain green, or brown. The body was green, or brown, with dark dorsal and subdorsal lines, thickly dotted all over with black-ringed white dots. The obliques were long, rather wide ovals of white edged with black, the edge being irregular. The horn was gone, and the tubercle was shining black encircled with deep yellow. The legs and props were of the body-color. There were more brown than green caterpillars.

Both species now ate voraciously and grew very rapidly. They are very satisfactory crawlers to rear, for they are not delicate, do not hurt each other, and have no unpleasant ways. Their boxes give out an agreeable odor, and the caterpillars " eat the leaves up clean," leaving only stems to be removed. When at rest the head and first two segments are drawn into the third segment, which is very much larger than any other. These are the most formidable caterpillars on woodbine or grape-vines, and they sometimes do real harm, because so many eggs may be laid on one vine, and each crawler eats so much that the vine is almost defoliated. We once saw half a peck of the two species taken from a woodbine which grew over a piazza, and we had to see this rich treasure thrown away, wasted, because we were visiting a family which shuddered at the mere mention of any crawling thing, and we could not, of course, take the caterpillars into the house. We have never ceased to regret the loss, however.

Pandorus fed for six days, *achemon* for five, after the fourth molt, then stopped eating, and crawled restlessly about the tins. Each larva was put into a separate smaller box to lie still and become a pupa. The green crawlers grew purplish on the dorsum, and the brown ones reddish or grayish, as they approached pupation. The largest ones were over four inches long, the smallest a little over three inches, and there were more large ones than small.

For six days both species lay in their tins, and on the sixth cast the caterpillar-skins and appeared as bright green, soft pupæ, showing the wing-covers and abdominal segments more plainly than anything else. In fifteen or twenty hours they had settled into bright chestnut-brown pupæ, about two and a half inches long, though *achemon* was a trifle shorter than *pan-*

dorus. Pandorus was noticeably stouter than *achemon* and had a rounder head. *Achemon's* head was much more distinct from the thorax and more slender, forming an easy mark by which to distinguish the two species. These pupæ are easily disturbed and writhe and roll over and over when touched, or even exposed to the air, at first. Later they become more quiet, but still move the abdomen when held in a warm hand. Out of doors the pupæ are formed in cells underground, but they do not need earth in tin boxes unless they exude more fluid than usual. One *achemon* larva spun a few threads of silk over a little earth which was in his tin — the only instance.

The moths are very beautiful, and very unlike in color. *Pandorus* has shades of rich olive-green, the dark shades being especially velvety. The fore wings have patches of pale pink, varying much in depth of color, and sometimes merely suggested. The hind wings have, each, a pale pink patch, a black patch, and some lines. The under side is of a yellower green. The antennæ are light above, rust-colored on the under side, and are ciliate in the male, while those of the female are simple.

Achemon has the head, thorax, and abdomen ashes-of-roses, the patagia velvety brown, the antennæ cream-colored above and rust-red beneath, and curved back at the tip. Those of the male are ciliate, those of the female simple. The fore wings are ashes-of-roses, with dark brown lines and spots; the hind wings pink at the base, having the margin ashes-of-roses, with a series of dark brown spots. The under side of both wings is rust-colored, flushed with pink.

These moths have tongues long enough to reach the nectar of Japanese honeysuckles, nasturtiums, and similar flowers, but not long enough for the deeper honeysuckles and day-lilies. They fly after dark, and have a very strong, rapid flight. They are eaten by several kinds of birds — blackbirds, robins, orioles, and even English sparrows.

The Other of Us was called down-stairs one day to "come and see an English sparrow waltzing on the lawn with a humming-bird." On reaching the lawn she found the sparrow trying to fly away with a fine *pandorus* moth, evidently not long out of the pupa, though its wings were dry and fully developed. She drove away the sparrow and put the moth in a safe place on a woodbine; but it did not stay there, and its fluttering along the ground soon drew the attention of the sparrows, and again one of them seized it, succeeded in detaching three of its wings, and flew away with the body and one wing before any one saw that the moth was in need of help.

Orioles, as well as sparrows, frequent woodbines and destroy many more moths and caterpillars than the noisy English sparrows, going quietly and systematically to work, examining every stem and leaf, and carrying to their young in the nest hundreds of *myron*, *achemon*, *pandorus*, *nessus*, and *abbotii* larvæ. Indeed, orioles are more destructive to more species of caterpillars than any other birds we have watched, for they eat and carry to their young the hairy *Clisiocampa*, or "tent-caterpillars," and eat the *Hyphantria cunea*, or "fall web-worms," in immense numbers, eating also the pupæ of the "forest tent-caterpillars," which they pull out of the cocoons after making a neat slit in the side of the cocoon at the "exit end." This makes them very valuable birds to have among us; but if we want woodbine sphingids, it is very trying to see orioles fly away with one after another, while we fail to find them in time to save them.

Pandorus and *achemon* are said to be double-brooded, but we have never found them earlier than July in any stage, and the pupæ formed from this brood have never given the moth in time for a second brood. Usually our moths have not emerged before the last of June or the first of July of the following year, but occasionally one has come out, when the house has been over-warmed with a furnace fire, in November or December. From early July until October, eggs, larvæ, and moths may be found, September being the best month, in New England, for half-grown and full-grown caterpillars.

AMPELOPHAGA CHŒRILUS

GENUS,   AMPELOPH'AGA (" vine-eater," though it does not eat Ampelopsis).
SPECIES, CHŒR'ILUS.

The Lane furnished us with our eggs of *chœrilus*. One of Us searched the azalea and viburnum, and found on the under side of the leaves globular green eggs, which hatched in six days.

The caterpillars were very pale green, with long black horns which turned backward and were bifid at the tip. After eating their egg-shells they ate round holes through the leaves. In a few days they grew glassy green, with paler green lateral lines, and the horns became brown, lighter at base on the sides and back. They rested on the midrib of the leaf.

Four days after hatching they molted. They were green, with faint white lateral and oblique lines, and brown horns. The spiracles were faint orange, not noticeable.

Six days later they molted again, and lost the glassy look. The lateral lines disappeared on the fourth segment, and were lacking on all between that and the tenth segment, where they reappeared. The body was very white between the obliques, which did not meet on the back. The dorsal area was covered with dots. The legs were light, and the feet had a

Ampelophaga chœrilus.

transparent look. The sides of the brown horn were lighter and reddish. The segments were very plainly marked, and the third and fourth were swollen. There were faint face-lines.

The third molt followed in five days. The caterpillars had very small heads, with whitish face-lines. The body was very yellow-green, with a faint dorsal line. The last pair of obliques were very white. The caudal horn was blue, with black granules. The feet were quite red, the spiracles bright red with a yellow dot at each end. Other larvæ had the horn blue at the base and light pink above.

The fourth molt occurred five days later. The head was marked by face-lines which continued over the first and second segments, much fainter on the second. The body was bluer green than in the last molt and darker below the lateral line. The obliques were much whiter. Some horns were very blue, others pinkish. Some larvæ were brown instead of green. The anal shield was edged with lighter green or brown, according to the body-color of the crawler. The swollen segments were very conspicuous and had no dots. The illustration shows one green and one brown caterpillar. They posed side by side as if for comparison.

Before pupating they turned pinkish on the dorsum, and, thirteen days after the fourth molt, began spinning leaves together with a " fish-net " cocoon. Three days later the pupæ cast the larva-skin, having lived thirty-six days from the egg. They ate *Azalea viscosa* and *Viburnum dentatum*, and ate from the margin of the leaf after the second molt.

We have not found *chœrilus* common, but have oc-

8

casionally come upon single caterpillars feeding on azalea in the swampy fields or by the edge of the Lane. We have never found an early moth or larva, ours being all in August and September. It is considered double-brooded and " rather common from Canada to Georgia, and westward to Iowa," according to Mr. Beutenmüller.

The pupa is pinkish brown speckled with black, and very deep brown between the segments. It is pinker than *myron*.

In the moth the head and thorax are of a deep cinnamon-brown, the abdomen being of a lighter and grayer shade. The fore wings are of a purple-brown, with greenish scales along the costa and a wide band of the deep cinnamon-brown crossing each wing near the apex. A narrow and broken band is sometimes found nearer the base of the wing. The fore wings are slightly falcate. The hind wings are of a very red tan-color, or rust-color, unmarked. The antennæ are tan-color on one side and white on the other. They are simple in the female and ciliate in the male. The tongue is not an inch long. The moths fly after dark.

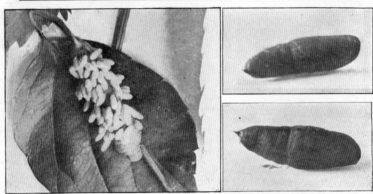

Ampelophaga myron (larva with cocoons of parasite).

AMPELOPHAGA MYRON

GENUS, AMPELOPH'AGA ("vine-eater").
SPECIES, MY'RON (named for the sculptor Myron).

In one of our morning walks up the Lane we spied a greenish moth on the under side of an oak-leaf. Holding a box under her, we broke off the stem and dropped leaf and moth into the box, covering it very quickly, for there is always a chance of losing the moth, though by day many sphingid moths are inactive — apparently asleep.

When we examined our captive it proved to be *myron*, the first one of its kind we had seen. Having learned the unwisdom of killing a moth before trying to get eggs from it, we put it into a box with netting over the top, and waited for the next day to show the result. Great was our delight on finding the netting and paper lining studded with almost globular bright apple-green eggs, and many of them. Putting the moth into a fresh box, we detached all the eggs, cutting the netting and paper when they did not come off easily, and counted ninety-three of the pretty things. These were shut into a little tin box, labeled and dated, and put on a shelf to wait for hatching-time. This was in June.

For six nights the *myron* laid eggs, fewer each night, until we had two hundred, then she died.

115

On the sixth day after they were laid the eggs began to turn yellow, and on the ninth day they hatched, giving little bright yellow caterpillars with long, curving caudal horns which soon turned black, and having short unnoticeable setæ. Two years later we had another lot of eggs, which hatched in six days after they were laid. This was in July. The egg-period is, therefore, not always the same, though one of six days is more common than one of nine.

The little caterpillars were given grape-leaves. They did not eat their shells, but drank thirstily, then began to eat the leaves, and grew greener as they ate. They were very active, and several escaped through a tiny crack where the corner of the box-cover did not fit perfectly, and in spite of wet scrim which was over the top of the box. This was our first proof that round-topped boxes were safer for young caterpillars.

The second brood had straight horns and were fed on woodbine.

The first brood molted six days, the second four days, after hatching. The first brood came out greener yellow, with deeper green below the white subdorsal line, which extended from head to horn. The abdominal segments were much whiter on the dorsum than the thoracic, and had a green mark, shaped like a two-tined pitchfork-iron, on each segment. The caudal horn was whitish at base, and reddish or purplish the rest of the way to the tip. The head and legs were green. The anal shield had a faint whitish edge. The third and fourth segments were larger on the sides than any of the others, a characteristic of this family, and specially marked in *myron*, which some of the children used to call "the broad-shoul-dered caterpillars," and other children "the big-sleeved caterpillars." In this stage, however, the tumidity was barely indicated, not really noticeable. The cater-pillars ate their skins, except the horns and masks.

The second molt followed in three days for the first brood, in four days for the second. This time the head had faint yellow face-lines, and all setæ disappeared. The body was bright green with paler dorsal areas, and the first brood had a red spot on the dorsal line of each abdominal segment. The second brood lacked these spots. Both had pink caudal horns and notice-able tumidity of the third and fourth segments.

The first brood molted again in four days, the sec-ond in three, and this time the crawlers were a little over an inch long, and had head, props, and body bright green granulated with yellow. The head had two yellow face-lines, and a lateral yellow line on each edge. The subdorsal line was yellow, and each ab-dominal segment had a dorsal red spot set in a yellow patch. There were seven oblique lines of yellow gran-ules set close together, and a faint sublateral yellow line on the first three segments. The spiracles were bright red, with a yellow dot at each end. The anal plate was edged with yellow. The horn was reddish. The swelling of the third and fourth segments was much increased.

The second brood molted for the fourth time three days later, but the first brood fed for six days before molting again. This time they were over an inch and a quarter in length, bright yellow-green on the dor-sum, blue-green below, and the granulation had become yellow dots, not raised. The head had bright yellow face-lines. The legs were green with red-brown tips, and each had a black spot. The props were green suffused with almost lilac. The anal shield was edged with yellow, and the horn was blue-green at the base, then yellow-green, then yellow at the tip, granulated with blue-black above and beneath, the yellow subdorsals extending part-way up the sides. The spiracles were red with a white dot at each end, except on the first segment, where the dots were clear yellow. The obliques were faint and lilac-whitish. In the first brood the caudal horn was purplish, bluish, or reddish, and there were dorsal red spots on the abdominal segments. These were lacking in the second brood. The third and fourth segments were much swollen.

The second brood gave still greater variety by showing several caterpillars of a clear yellow-brown color, with queer splashes of dark bottle-green, and obliques of pinkish lilac. One molted a very pink-brown, with pink obliques and subdorsals. In these varieties the horn was blackish green with yellow tips. Two of the larvæ had one red spot each, on the dorsum. They ate voraciously and grew to a length of about three inches.

On the fifth day the first brood, and on the sixth day the second brood, began to turn pink or pinkish lilac, and stopped eating, then spun loose webs among leaves, or fastened leaves to the tin. In three days the second brood cast the caterpillar-skin, but the first brood were quiet for seven days before the pupæ appeared.

The pupæ were of pale coffee-brown, suffused at

Ampelophaga myron.

first with pink, dotted with dark brown. The abdomen
was of lighter color than the rest, and had a very dark
band between each two segments. The pupæ were
one and three eighths inches long, not slender, and had
a sharp cremaster.

The moths of the second brood, which had pupated
in August, emerged in September, twenty-two days
later, while the pupæ of the first brood, formed in
July, did not give the moths until May of the following year.

Three years later we had three sets of *myron* eggs
from captured moths. Of these three broods nearly
half the larvæ were of shades of brown, varying from
a clear, light tan to a deep chocolate-brown, with pinkish obliques edged below with dark brown or dark
green, and the bodies were spotted with either dark
brown or dark green. All these had red spots on the
dorsum.

It is not uncommon for a species to show two forms
of coloring, the brown and the green, and often there are
intermediate forms combining both colors; but one's
first experience of it is always a surprise. If some
hatched brown and others green it would not seem so
queer, but having them alike until the third or fourth
molt and then so very different is startling until one
is used to it.

Myron is one of our most common caterpillars in
New England, and is found on grape and woodbine
only, as far as records show, and we have never succeeded in making it eat any other leaf. It is found
"from Canada to Georgia, and westward to Missouri
and Iowa," Mr. Beutenmüller says. There is a variety,

cnotus, rare in the North, but the common form in the South. It differs from *myron* in having the fore wings brown instead of green and gray-green. Both have the hind wings of a bright tan-color, *myron's* having a green patch at the anal angle.

In *myron* the body is gray-green, the patagia being of the brighter green of the wing-patches. The antennæ are pale above and tawny beneath, and the legs are gray-green. The tongue is about an inch long. The moths fly rather early after dark, and are easy to net.

The caterpillars feed on cloudy days nearly all day, and on sunny days begin to feed toward sunset. They rest on the stem or midrib of the leaf when nearly full grown, and bite the edge, so that the head only is seen, unless one can go behind the vine, as on a piazza or trellis. All these caterpillars make a slight noise in eating, and we have often found them by hearing this. The very young caterpillars cling to any vein of a young leaf, and eat holes in the parenchyma, or green part, until they are big enough to hold the edge of the leaf and bite through the whole tissue.

Orioles are very destructive to them, and search our vine by the hour, carrying off to their young many a fine specimen which we would gladly have if it were within reach. Gray squirrels also eat them with eagerness.

Myron caterpillars, when full grown or nearly so, are more quiet than *abbotii* or *inscripta*, having none of the petulant jerking motion when disturbed, and it may be because of this that they are so often stung by brac'onid flies. The fly pierces the caterpillar's skin

with its ovipositor and lays several eggs in the caterpillar's body. We have counted seventy cocoons on
one poor *myron*. From the eggs hatch tiny grubs,
which feed upon the tissues of the caterpillar until
they are full fed, when they eat their way through its
skin, holding firmly to the larva by their anal end, and
in this position spin their little white cocoons. Many
a caterpillar bristling with these cocoons has been
brought to us as a rare specimen! Most persons who
see one like this for the first time think that the
cocoons are eggs. Only flies will hatch from such a
specimen, and there is no way of saving its life.

Experience enables us to tell a stung specimen before the grubs come out to spin. There is a peculiar
look about the caterpillar, and when the grubs are
nearly full fed they can be seen moving about under
the skin of their host. The presence of these braconid
flies is one of the most trying calamities an entomologist has to bear.

Myron is said to be double-brooded, but we find
moths, eggs, and larvæ from May till October.

IX

SUBFAMILY SPHINGINÆ

SUBFAMILY, SPHINGI'NÆ.

PROTOPARCE CELEUS

GENUS,   PROTOPAR'CE.
SPECIES, CE'LEUS (a king of Eleusis).

WE hunted for these eggs on the tomato-plants, and found plenty on the under side of leaves, one or two eggs to a leaf, never more. They were globular, and exactly of the leaf-color, and were probably recently laid, for it was four or five days before they grew yellowish, and six before the first one hatched. The little caterpillar was not quite a quarter of an inch long, green, with sparse setæ, and a dark gray, long, slender caudal horn which curved backward.

In five days the first molt came, and the larvæ had doubled in length. The head was smaller in proportion to the body, round, green, and granulated. The body was green, with transverse rows of granulations, denser on the first three segments. The legs were gray, the props green, and the caudal horn was dark gray, slender, and curved backward. The spiracles, usually inconspicuous at this early stage of larval life, were plainly visible and dark gray.

Protoparce celeus.

These caterpillars were rather quiet and gave no trouble, eating well, but not voraciously. Four days later they molted again, and again were doubled in length, being three quarters of an inch long. The head was green, rough with white granules, and the mouth-parts were gray. The body was just the green of a tomato-leaf — of the under side — and had a broad white subdorsal band from head to horn. Seven faint yellow obliques showed. The horn was long, slender, straight, green above and beneath, with black spines, and white on the sides with white spines, the tip ending in two black spines. The legs were green, ringed with gray, the props green, and the anal plate was edged with white. The spiracles were gray encircled with white.

The third molt took place in five days. The crawlers were not quite an inch and a quarter long. They were of the deeper green of the upper side of the leaf now, granulated, and on the thoracic segments the granules were sharp like thorns, each set in a circle of darker green. The obliques were yellow-white, the last pair wider than the others and extending up the sides of the caudal horn, which was almost black above and beneath. The anal plate was edged with yellow-white. The legs were gray, with white thorns on the outer, and black dashes on the inner, side. The props were green granulated with white. The spiracles were deep orange, surrounded by a black line, then by a gray band, except on the first segment, where they were buff with no rings.

The fourth molt followed in three days. The crawlers were nearly two inches long and began to eat ravenously. They had changed somewhat. The head was large, round, pale green with a few white dots. The first and anal segments were like the head. The thoracic segments and the dorsum and venter of all were dotted with white. The abdominal segments were dark blue-green with transverse striations. The obliques were yellow-white, the last half of the last pair being clear white. On the substigmatal ridge was a pale green line which made a $\angle$ with each oblique, inclosing the spiracle. The spiracles were white on the first segment, buff on the others, and encircled with black. The anal plate was edged with greenish yellow. The caudal horn was long, slender, sharp, rough, and blue-black, with a few white spines. The legs were green with black dashes, the props were green dotted with white, the anal pair paler.

The caterpillars ate so much that in five days they grew to a length of four and a quarter inches, being as large around as a forefinger, and very strong. They jerked themselves furiously if disturbed, and made a squeaking noise, but how they made it we never could find out. The boxes can be kept clean much more easily at this stage if a little sand is sprinkled on the bottom.

At the end of the five days they stopped eating, grew duller in color, and crawled noisily about the tins, trying to get out. We found that they exuded so much sticky fluid that we gave them a little earth in the tins. They went into this — it was not more than two inches deep — and lay there for two weeks. Then the pupæ appeared, bright green in color, soft, and with a short, wide flap from the head over the wing-covers. We left them to harden, when, to our surprise, they had long loops from the head to beyond the middle of the wing-covers, like jug-handles.

After this One or the Other of Us was on the watch to see a pupa just out of the larva-skin, and observe its development into the brown, firm pupa with the "jug-handle" tongue-case. It was a long time before success rewarded our vigilance, but at last One of Us, who had prepared a box with only earth enough to absorb the fluid from the caterpillar without being deep enough to cover it, saw a pupa wriggling out of the larva-skin. At first it was a green, pulpy mass, with the abdominal segments very soft and stretched out, the eyes very prominent, and the head bent forward over the thorax, while the tongue-case was double, short, wide, flat, and appressed. Very slowly the body contracted into shape, the head drew back into line with the body, and the tongue-case, now looking like a single tube, "pulled" out like molasses candy, becoming more slender, with a bulbous tip, just as a bit of molasses candy does when pulled. As the head drew back and the body contracted, the tongue was left in the air, except where its tip touched the wing-covers, and its base was attached to the head. Still it was not arched like the tongue-cases of the other pupæ, but sagged in the middle or just below it. In time, however, as the membrane covering it grew firmer, it rose into a fine curve and hardened, growing brown as did the rest of the pupa. This process occupied two hours, and even then the color was not the deep chestnut-brown which it became later. The wing-covers were drawn out to their full size in the same way.

The pupæ were a little over two and a half inches long, and the tip of the tongue-case touched the wing-covers a little more than half-way down.

They are very easily injured at first, and the prominent tongue-case breaks so easily that great care is needed in packing these pupæ for transportation. Fine, sifted earth is the best packing, though cotton may be used if no pressure comes on the tongue-case.

The caterpillars feed on tomato, tobacco, potato, *Datura* (jimson-weed), ground-cherry, and matrimony-vine, and a great deal they eat, too. When hatched they eat little holes through a leaf; then as they grow they begin on a very tender young leaf at the top of a stem of tomato, for instance, strip the midrib completely on both sides, and then take the next larger leaf. They feed at dusk, night, and early morning, hiding through the day, unless it is cloudy or rainy, or they are molting or stung.

They may be traced by following the bare midribs and stems — for in the later molts they devour the midribs too — and searching the leaves nearest the last bare stem, counting from the top. The balls of excrement also show where the caterpillar has been or is, and sharp eyes do the rest. The green crawlers are not easy to find. We have seen an observing man look carefully over a whole plant and fail to find two half-grown ones which we could see all the time. One of Us was quite indignant with the Other for showing her as a caterpillar what she supposed to be a green tomato. It was both. At least, it was a *celeus* and part of the tomato, the rest being inside *celeus*, who lay in the hollow he had eaten out of the tomato and looked just like it. It was only his moving head which be-

Protoparce celeus. Pupæ of celeus and carolina for comparison.

trayed him to the Other of Us. For these big and voracious crawlers eat leaves and green and ripe tomatoes
with equal enjoyment after reaching the third or fourth
molt, though, as they cannot see, they do not select the
best tomatoes, as birds and wasps choose the best pears.

We had been told of " huge black " caterpillars on
tomato-plants, and had seen records of " a dark form "
of *celeus*, but we could not find one for many years.
Then one day a man came to the piazza on his bicycle,
and handed us a tin coffee-can, saying, " I thought you
might like these, and the folks was glad to be quit of
them." One of Us opened the box and poured out
two or three full-grown *celeus* larvæ, then a "huge
black " one, then two or three of a deep purple-brown
color, then two which looked like green overshot with
brown, as silk is sometimes. In all there were sixteen
big crawlers, and not one bit of food for them. Tomato-
leaves were soon provided, and the caterpillars were
sorted according to color. The next day One of Us
found several brown *celeus* and one almost black one
in the doctor's garden, and then we were satisfied. It
is so much more satisfactory to find them one's self !

The " black" and brown ones are marked like the
green ones, and their pupæ are not to be distinguished
from those of the green larvæ.

It is much easier to see the dark caterpillars on the
vines, for they are very conspicuous, but when they
crawl about on the ground before burrowing they
have a better chance of escaping notice than the green
ones. We followed a green *celeus* once when it left
the tomato-vine, to see how far it would go before
burrowing. The ground was soft all about, after
celeus crossed one path, yet the creature crawled

seventy-five or eighty feet without stopping, simply going straight in the direction in which it had started. Then, when it began to burrow, One of Us picked it up and put it into a tin.

The moths are handsome, very large and very strong, and have tongues fully four inches long. They are dusk-fliers, and frequent honeysuckle, lilies, and other sweet flowers having long tubes. They are all gray, black, and white, except a row of orange spots on each side of the abdomen. Like most sphingid moths, they dart downward when frightened, so a net should be held below the moth to be caught. This habit is to be remembered when transferring the moth from the net to the cage. If the opening of the cage is uppermost, the net can be brought down, opened just enough to give the moth room to pass, and it will dart down into the cage.

These moths are said to be double-brooded, but we have never found eggs or caterpillars earlier than late July, though we have caught the moths early in July. Farther south there are probably two broods each year. They are rather common all over the United States and Canada — in some places very common, in others much less so.

The pupæ are often turned up when potatoes are dug or gardens are "spaded over."

Robins have been seen carrying off full-grown *celeus* caterpillars, having first pecked them till they loosened their hold of the tomato-stems and fell to the ground, where they were soon reduced to helplessness by the robins. We have not known or heard of any other bird's attempting to eat them.

Protoparce carolina (half grown).

PROTOPARCE CAROLINA

GENUS,   PROTOPAR'CE.
SPECIES,   CAROLI'NA.

Carolina is a more Southern species than *celeus,* or rather is more common in the South than elsewhere, although it is found all over the United States and in Canada. It feeds on tomato, potato, tobacco, and *Datura stramonium,* or jimson-weed.

We had more than one hundred eggs from the tomato-plants in the garden, and close examination showed that some were globular and the others ovoid, so we separated them and waited for the little crawlers to hatch. Fully half of the eggs turned speckled, then gray, then coal-black, and the upper part of the shell sank to the under part, giving a withered look. These eggs proved spoiled in some way and were thrown out. The rest were bright green, just the color of the tomato-leaves, and grew yellower and paler before hatching. They were laid on either the upper or under side of the leaf, and seldom more than one on a leaf. When more than one are found they may be laid by different moths. Some of the eggs found had no depression in the upper side, a sign of their being "fresh laid." These hatched on the seventh day, while others hatched in four, five, and six days after we found them — or the children, for two of the children helped us hunt for them. The globular eggs proved *celeus*, and their caterpillars have been described separately. The ovoid eggs gave *carolina*, but we did not know this until the crawlers were almost full fed, though we hoped for *carolina*. There are so many varieties of color and marks in *celeus* that we did not feel sure that these were not merely forms which we had not seen before, but we kept their history separate, hoping for *carolina*.

The newly hatched caterpillars were yellow, very pale and empty-looking, with straight reddish caudal horns. After eating their shells they began eating little holes through the leaves, and soon grew green, with a white subdorsal line from head to horn, while the horn became brown at base, shading lighter to the tip.

The young *celeus* had a dark gray horn which curved backward.

In four days *carolina* molted for the first time, and the head was round, green, and rough with white granules. The body was green, with white dots and white subdorsals from head to horn. *Celeus* had no subdorsals, or very faint ones.

In *carolina* the horn was dark brown, lighter at the tip, very large at the base, but tapering rapidly to a very slender upper part, and rough with short spines. The next day white obliques appeared, crossing the subdorsals and almost meeting on the dorsal line. The larvæ ate their skins. *Celeus* still had the horn gray.

The second molt came three days later. The head

was almost round, green, with white granules. The body was green, with white granules on the thoracic and white dots on the abdominal segments, white subdorsals, and white obliques edged above with black. The legs were dark, the props green; the anal plate was edged with light yellow-green. The horn was brown at base, almost black at tip, and rough with dark spines. The crawlers ate their skins, except the masks.

Celeus had the horn green in front and behind with black spines, and white on the sides with white spines, and the legs green ringed with gray.

Four days later they molted for the third time. The head was round and green, finely dotted with white. The body was green, with white granules on the tho-racic segments, and dots on the lower part of the abdominal segments. The dorsum was very white-green, the sides were very yellow-green, and the ventral and stigmatal areas were very blue-green. These shades of green varied enough to give a striped look to the caterpillars, very different from the blue-green or yellow-green or white-green of *celeus* larvæ, each of which was of one shade. *Carolina's* obliques were white, edged above with black; *celeus'* were yellow-white. *Carolina's* legs were green and black; *celeus'* were gray and black. *Carolina's* props were green, and the anal plate was edged with bright yellow-green. *Carolina's* horn was bright tan-color, with black spines in front and behind, long and stout. *Celeus'* horn was either black, blue with black spines, blue at the sides and black in front and behind, or black with white part-way up the sides.

The caterpillars ate voraciously for a week, then molted for the fourth time. *Carolina* now showed three distinct forms — one just like the last molt, except that the horn was red, shorter in proportion, and curved backward. The second had a plain green head; the body green, minutely dotted with white, and with the obliques white, edged above with broken black lines. The legs were black and white, looking speckled; the props were green; the anal plate was edged with yellow-green. The horn was short, stout, rose-red. The third form was of a dirty green, the head plain, the body transversely striated, or finely lined, with black, and with white dots so small as to be seen with a lens only. The obliques were dirty white, with black above. The legs were black and dirty white, the props dirty green; the anal plate was edged with dull yellow. The horn was short, stout, and dull red.

There was a fourth form much like the last, but the green was more olive on the head, and there were two broad face-lines of smoky black. The body had a black dorsal line, somewhat broken, and was of a cleaner green, with a black patch on the dorsum of the first segment. The legs were black and green, the props green with black marks; the horn was short, stout, and red. The spiracles of all were black, with a yellowish dot at each end, in a gray oval.

No *carolina* had the shining look which the green forms of *celeus* have when nearly full fed, but all were dull of surface, and the dorsum was set with many short pale brown setæ, the sides having fewer.

They fed for ten days, then stopped eating and crawled restlessly until they grew moist, shortened,

and lay on the earth provided to absorb the fluid ex·
uding from them at this stage. The earth was not
deep enough for burrowing, and the pupation could
be watched as far as outer changes were concerned.
In eight days the pupæ cast the larva-skin, and were
green, becoming chestnut-brown far more quickly than
celeus pupæ. They are shorter and smaller than *celeus*
pupæ, and have the tongue-case much shorter, less
curved, and touching the wing-covers less than half-
way down.

Celeus larvæ, after the fourth molt, vary in almost
every way except the shape of the obliques ∠, the
chief point distinguishing them from *carolina*, as the
red horn of *carolina* is usually given as the distinctive
mark of that crawler. Whatever the shade of brown,
black, olive, or green of the *celeus* larva, each oblique
is always supplemented by a horizontal line at the
lower end, making a ∠ with the oblique line. This
is not the case with *carolina*. *Celeus* larvæ have
great variety of color in their spiracles, too, some being
black in white oval lines; others tan-colored, with a
dark dot in the middle and a white or a black line
around the edge; others orange, with a yellow-white
dot at each end, in a white oval or in a gray one.

In our experience, the horn of *carolina* is the first
distinguishing mark, but we confess that, so great is
the variety in the coloring of *celeus*, we should not be
overwhelmed with surprise if some day we found a
celeus with a red horn.

The *carolina* moth is much browner and darker than
celeus, and the orange spots on the abdomen are
larger than those of *celeus*, while its general effect is

more mottled and less streaked. The moths fly at dusk and later, and may be caught near honeysuckles, phlox, lilies, and electric lights. They have great strength of wing-muscles and a quick, powerful flight. Their tongues are very long. The male's antennæ are biciliate, while the female's are simple. In some places they are double-brooded, but we have not found any June brood in spite of all our searching. With us, in Massachusetts and Vermont, both *carolina* and *celeus* moths have been found from July till late September, and the eggs or caterpillars from late July until the very end of October, without the interval there would be if there were two broods. Occasionally a moth has emerged from our pupæ in November or December, but too late for another brood.

Protoparce carolina (tongue).

SPHINX KALMIÆ

GENUS, SPHINX.
SPECIES, KAL'MIÆ ("of laurel").

"Sphinx" because the caterpillars rear the fore part of the body and rest in a position which Linnæus thought suggestive of the sphinx, and "kalmiæ" because the caterpillars were first found on laurel, *Kalmia latifolia*. We have found them on lilac, ash, beach-plum, and fringe-tree, and others mention privet as their food-plant. They also are said to be double-brooded, but we have found the caterpillars only in August, September, and October, and the moths never emerged in the same year.

Their range is from Canada to Georgia, and west to Missouri, but they are not common. It is an event to find the larva, and we have caught but few of the female moths. One laid us eggs on the 3d of September — very pale green, oval eggs, which hatched seven days later, in the afternoon, having turned sordid white the day before.

The young caterpillars were three sixteenths of an inch long, and colorless until they ate, except the caudal horn, which was gray and curved forward. After feeding they were green, except the head, anal segment, legs, and props, which were yellowish, and the

135

gray horn, which was darkest at the tip. The horn was slender, smooth, blunt at the tip, and almost as long as the caterpillar. The setæ were sparse. The larvæ did not eat their shells.

In three days they molted, and were half an inch long, slender and green. The head was round, bilobed, and green. The body was green, with a lateral white line and a faint stigmatal one from the head to the anal shield. The setæ were sparse. The legs and props were green, the spiracles indistinct. The horn was long, sharp, green at base, brown above, and rough with black thorns or spines. There were seven pairs of faint white obliques, the last pair wider and whiter than the others.

The second molt followed in four days, with little increase of length. The head was green, and rough with yellow granules. The body was green, with yellow granules, more numerous on the dorsum. There was a yellow lateral line from head to horn. The obliques were yellow. On the fourth segment, close above the oblique, was a very noticeable large blue-black dot. The caudal horn was green, with a black tip and black spines. The legs and props were green. A few days later yellow face-lines appeared, and faint blue-black lines above some of the obliques. The thoracic and anal segments were thickly dotted, rather than granulated, with yellow. The legs gained a reddish brown dot on each.

On the fourth day they molted for the third time, and were one and one eighth inches long. The head was now broader at the bottom than at the top, slightly bilobed, green, with yellowish face-lines, and lightly granulated. The body was green, slightly granu-

Sphinx kalmiæ.

lated with yellow on the dorsum,— more so on the sublateral area,— while the thoracic segments were granulated all over and had a line of yellow granules. The anal shield and props were speckled with blue-black. The horn was green, black at the tip, rough with blue-black thorns, long, turned backward, and sharp. The spiracles were orange, and the obliques yellow edged above with blue-black. The legs were green, ringed with white and black, and the props green, with a blue-black band.

Before the fourth molt they fed for six days, then molted, coming out an inch and three quarters long. The head was smooth, green, with face-lines of light green and black. The body was smooth, light green on the back and darker elsewhere. The anal shield was speckled with black. The obliques were very bright yellow, edged above with blue-black. The legs were green, with white and black at the tips, the props green with black bands, and the spiracles orange.

A second brood had the first molt in six days from hatching, the second in three, the third in eleven, and the fourth in seven. These caterpillars differed slightly from the first brood. They had a line of white between the yellow and blue-black of the obliques, and their horns were blue-green at the base, glassy yellow-green behind, and whitish green in front, but changed later to blue-green.

Both broods fed for seven days after the last molt, then stopped eating. The caterpillars were three and three eighths inches long, having grown to this length from one and one half inches in one week. They grew very yellow-green.

The pupæ were found in a few days,— less than a

week,— and were one and three quarters inches long, neither stout nor slender, and of a deep wine-color, lighter between the segments and around the wing-covers. They had short tongue-cases, whose slightly bulbous tips just touched the thorax. Out of doors these caterpillars burrow in the earth to pupate, but ours transformed perfectly on the bottom of their tins without any earth.

The moths are in shades of brown, white, and black, the general effect being brown. The head, thorax, and abdomen are chestnut-brown above, lighter beneath. The patagia are edged with black. The abdomen has a narrow black dorsal line, and black sides with a row of large whitish spots on each. The fore wings are light chestnut-brown, with dark and lighter marks and white and black cross-lines. The hind wings are brownish white, with a black band across the middle and one across the outer margin of each.

We have seen the moths ovipositing in the dusk, flying from one lilac-twig to another and fastening a shining green egg to the under side of a leaf here and there, never laying many eggs on one bush, but darting away to the nearest lilac, laying a few eggs on its leaves, then leaving it for another bush.

If eggs or larvæ are found on a bush or tree, it is a good plan to examine the nearest trees or bushes of the same kind, as more eggs may be found in this way. It is much more satisfactory to have eggs or very young caterpillars, for older *kalmiæ* are often stung by parasitic flies.

The moths may be taken at light or bait, but are not common.

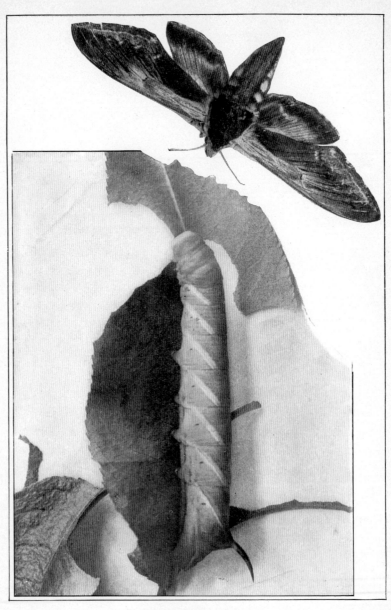

Sphinx drupiferarum.

SPHINX DRUPIFERARUM

GENUS, SPHINX.

SPECIES, DRUPIFERA'RUM ("of drupe-bearing trees").

This is not a common caterpillar, and when found in autumn on wild-cherry, plum, apple, or hackberry trees is usually stung. Once in a long while one is found crawling on the ground, searching for a good place to burrow, and this one may give a fine moth, or may be stung, or may die in the pupa-case from any one of several causes. Perhaps more caterpillars, and unstung ones, might be found by taking a lantern and searching the trees after dark, for "good" *drupiferarum* larvæ evidently do not feed by day, or even rest on the stems, leaves, or twigs where we can find them. We have never tried the lantern experiment, but it may be worth trying, notwithstanding. We have had several larvæ which gave us moths, but never a moth which gave us eggs, and our history is the life-story of just one caterpillar, whose egg was found on the under side of a wild-cherry leaf in July.

Two eggs were found on the same sapling, and were very nearly alike in size, shape, and color, being ovoid and pale green, of just the color of the leaf surface on which they were found. One egg hatched a day before the other and gave a little crawler which

grew into a fine red-spotted *myops* and became a pupa
before *drupiferarum* had molted for the fourth time.
But at first the two little crawlers were much alike.
They had round pale green heads, slender pale green
bodies with yellowish subdorsal lines, and lateral lines
on the thoracic segments. Their horns were slender,
of medium length, pale red, and rough.

Four days after hatching, *drupiferarum* molted.
The head was green, round, granulated with pale yellow. The body was green granulated with pale yellow, and had faint subdorsal, lateral, and oblique lines
of yellowish granules. The horn was red, the legs and
props were green, the anal plate was edged with
yellow.

Eight days later it molted again. The head was less
round, was green, and had yellow granules and face-
lines. The body was apple-green, with bright yellow
subdorsal lines, yellow lateral lines on the thoracic
segments, yellow obliques, edge of anal plate, and
granules. The general effect was very yellow rather
than green. The legs were green with red tips, the
props were green, and the horn was bright carmine
and rough.

In five days the third molt occurred. The head was
not quite round, and was apple-green with sharp yellow granules and faint yellow face-lines. The body
was apple-green with sharp granules of bright yellow,
and obliques of yellow granules with a very narrow,
faint line of mauve on their upper edge. The spiracles
were red but not conspicuous, the legs yellow with red
tips, the props green. The anal plate was edged with
bright yellow. The horn was red, long, and stout,

with red and yellow granules. The general effect was
red and yellow. The larva ate its skin after molting.

A week later it molted for the fourth time. The head
was deep green, with a wide purple-brown stripe on
each side, and was very smooth. The body was smooth,
yellow-green dotted with yellow, with white obliques
edged above with mauve. The legs were yellow, with
red-brown tips; the props green, with a yellow line
above the planta of each. The anal plate was edged
with yellow. The horn was long, very stout, curving
backward, smooth, red-brown, almost black at tip, with
a black line up the front, and yellow from the last pair
of obliques on the base behind. The spiracles were
orange and not conspicuous. Three days later the
thoracic segments were clear yellow-green without
dots, and the abdominal segments showed fewer dots
than before.

The crawler now ate voraciously, and had three
ways of treating leaves. It would begin at the tip and
eat down to the base on one side of the midrib; or it
would begin about an inch from the tip, eat in to the
midrib and then down in a curve nearly to the base
of the leaf, then treat the other side in the same way,
leaving a leaf-tip shaped like an arrow-head, and a
ragged base; or it would begin at the base and eat all
the leaf from one side of the midrib, and leave the
other side whole or but partly eaten.

It was a very quiet larva, never jerking or twitching,
and devoted itself to the business of feeding. It preferred the younger leaves of wild cherry — not choke-
cherry — to the last of its leaf-eating life, but would
eat older leaves if the younger ones were not to be had.

Its favorite positions were vertical, on a stem or leaf, as in the photograph, or hanging head downward on a pendent leaf, with the anal props clasping the leaf-stem. This latter is a position for feeding rather than for resting. In another feeding-position the anal props were on the twig, while the feet held the tip of a leaf bent down to the crawler's mandibles, the abdominal props, or part of them, holding the lower part of the midrib of the leaf.

Drupiferarum fed for nine days and then went into a tin with a little earth on the bottom to pupate. The pupa was freed from the larva-skin on August 26, forty-one days after the caterpillar left the egg.

The pupa was two and a quarter inches long, not stout, and of a deep purple-brown color. The abdominal segments were densely pitted; the wing-covers were very rough; the tongue-case was five sixteenths of an inch long, very slightly bulbous at tip, and appressed to the thorax for its whole length. The abdomen ended in a triangular, pointed tip. It was not an excitable pupa, though it would wriggle when held in a warm hand.

The moths are smoky black, gray, and brown, with whitish bands, black dashes, and white spots on the sides of the abdomen. They are much duller and grayer than *kalmiæ*, and larger. Their distinguishing mark is the whitish space along the costa on the fore wings. They fly after dark, and are powerful, swift moths. They are found from Canada to Florida, and in the West, but are common nowhere. Mr. Beutenmüller finds them double-brooded near New York, but we think them single-brooded in New England.

Sphinx gordius.

SPHINX GORDIUS

GENUS, SPHINX.
SPECIES, GOR'DIUS (the king who tied the Gordian knot).

This is a very variable species as far as the caterpillars are concerned, and any one finding the deep wine-colored form on low whortleberry- and blueberry-bushes would hardly recognize it as perhaps of the same brood with the bright green form on the neighboring sweet-fern.

One of Us found eggs on bayberry — green, ovoid eggs, which hatched three days later. The head of the little caterpillar was large and round. Its body was very light green without marks, and its caudal horn was black, erect, and short, brown at base · in front and behind, and light at the sides. The body was covered with short setæ, which were more noticeable on the anal shield than elsewhere. The segments were transversely striated, and the head and anal shield were of lighter color than the body. Three days later the head and thoracic segments were yellow-green, the abdominal segments, to the tenth, were blue-green, and the rest of the body was of a yellow-green, lighter than that of the head and thoracic segments. A dark dorsal line and lateral lines appeared, and the dorsum had a mottled look. The little cater-

143

pillars ate their shells and drank water eagerly. They rested on the upper side of the leaf, on the midrib.

The first molt occurred eight days after hatching, and the larvæ ate their skins except the masks. The head was large and round. The body was bright green, granulated with whitish, and had a dark dorsal line, while the lateral lines were whitish. The obliques showed faintly. The horn was dark brown, light at base except in front, and set thickly with spines. Two days later the granulations became yellow. The legs and mouth-parts were pinkish.

A week from the first molt came the second. The head was plain green. The body was yellow-green, very rough with granules, and had a lateral line and obliques of yellow granules, the obliques meeting on the dorsal line, the last pair being edged above with a little brown near the horn. The horn was brown, lighter at the base, and very spiny. Two days later the obliques were faintly edged with reddish brown, and the lateral line was visible on the thoracic segments only. The horn and legs became red.

Six days later the third molt took place. The head was pointed and very yellow-green, with yellow face-lines; the thoracic segments were yellow-green, and the rest of the body was apple-green, whiter below, thickly covered with yellow granules. The anal shield was edged with yellow. The horn was reddish and very rough. The obliques were clearly edged above with violet. A week later the granules were all white, except on the thoracic segments and anal shield. The horn was redder, and the obliques were yellow edged

Sphinx gordius.

above with white, then with crimson. The head was very dark yellow-green.

The fourth molt followed the third in eight days. The head was green, with yellowish face-lines edged with deep red-brown, not pointed, but not round. The body was apple-green covered with white dots, each dot encircled by a black ring, except near the obliques, where the rings were not found. The legs were reddish. The horn was short, stout, green above and beneath, black on the sides. The obliques were white edged above with crimson, which was darkest at the outer edge.

The caterpillars began to eat at the top of a spray of leaves, never left one leaf until all was eaten, then took the next leaf below.

When full fed the caterpillars were very blue-green, with white, black-ringed dots everywhere except on the anal segment in front of the horn. The body was lighter green on the dorsum. The spiracles were orange, with a yellow line around each. The legs were light red, the props dark green, the obliques white edged above with pale crimson, then deep crimson, with a hair-line of black at the upper edge. The head was large, dull green, with light green face-lines edged with brownish green.

The caterpillars varied in size and color, those described above being the most common form. Others were of a deep olive-green color, overlaid with wine-color, especially on the back, with the obliques of white, crimson, and almost black. Others were of a deep wine-color, the exact shade of the whortleberry-

10

leaves in autumn, with the obliques of a paler shade of the same color, and black caudal horns. All had the white dots set in the black rings.

These caterpillars are subject to diseases which kill many out of doors, and many more fall victims to several kinds of parasitic flies.

They fed for six days after the fourth molt, then stopped eating, went into the shallow earth provided for them, and in six days more the pupæ cast the larva-skin. The pupæ were dark brown, with short tongue-cases detached.

The food-plants of *gordius* are apple, pear, ash, bay-berry, blueberry, whortleberry, *Andromeda ligustrina*, and sweet-fern.

The moth is gray, black, and white, the fore wings having some sooty-brown color. The hind wings are white, with a band of black across the middle and a wider band along the outer edge. Hind wings so banded are common among the sphinx moths. The tongue is nearly two inches long. The moths fly after dark.

Sphinx luscitiosa.

SPHINX LUSCITIOSA

GENUS,   SPHINX.
SPECIES,   LUSCITIO'SA.

We never had the eggs of this rare moth. We caught a much-rubbed male flying over a field of rape at whose flowers it was feeding, and we could identify it very easily because it was so different from any of our other sphinx moths. Its fore wings were smoky brown, blacker on the costa and outer margin, and the hind wings were deep ocher-yellow, almost orange, with a wide black margin and a faint black band across each wing. We found no female then, but later our one caterpillar became a fine large female moth, larger than the male and having the wings grayer. The yellow of her hind wings was very grayish yellow.

It was near the rape-field that we found the caterpillar, a slender little one, only three quarters of an inch long, feeding on a poplar by the roadside. Its head was triangular, pale green, with pale yellow face-lines. The body was green, densely covered with white granules on the dorsum, but less so below the subdorsal lines. There was a bright yellow lateral line on the thoracic segments, extending faintly from there to the caudal horn. The obliques were pale yellow edged above with deep green, the last pair ex-

147

tending to the tip of the horn. The anal shield was edged with white and was bluer than any other part of the body. The legs and props were green; the caudal horn was pinkish in front and green behind. The spiracles were inconspicuous.

It molted four days later, and was unchanged, but after two days faint red lines appeared above the obliques, the tips of the legs became red, and the yellow face-lines were very bright.

It molted again in four days, the only change being a faint black edge added to the face-lines; but two days later, as often happens with sphinx caterpillars, the colors changed somewhat. The face-lines became pale green edged with faint black lines; the obliques were white edged above with pinkish lilac; the horn became green with a black stripe on each side; and the legs were white with red tips. The yellow lateral line disappeared from the thoracic segments. The props showed a faint purplish tinge. The spiracles were red. The thoracic segments and the lower parts of the other segments were covered with tiny white dots encircled by black rings. The horn was short in proportion to the size of the caterpillar. From this time the crawler ate voraciously and grew fast, and ten days later, when it stopped eating, it was three and a half inches long.

In this stage *luscitiosa* is often mistaken for *gordius*, especially when found on bayberry or blueberry. One entomologist wrote to the Other of Us that he found on bayberry a larva he supposed to be *gordius*, but the pupa gave *luscitiosa* in the spring, to his very great surprise. Willow and poplar are the usual food-plants reported for *luscitiosa*, but we have found larvæ on bayberry, blueberry, and *Andromeda ligustrina* within three years, as well as on *Prinos lævigata.*

Out of doors the caterpillars burrow in the earth to pupate, but pupate perfectly on the bottom of their tins in the Crawlery. The pupa is of a bright mahogany-color, with a short raised tongue-case extending about three sixteenths of an inch down the thorax.

The caterpillars are often stung by braconid flies, and very thoroughly stung, too, being covered with the cocoons when the parasitic larvæ come out to spin. This seems a great waste. We can bear having *myron* stung now and then, and rejoice when the tent-caterpillars fall victims to parasites; but when *luscitiosa* or *astylus* or *Dolba hylæus* is found dotted with eggs, or breaks out with cocoons, the disappointment and sense of loss are very great.

The range of *luscitiosa* is not yet known.

SPHINX CHERSIS

GENUS, SPHINX.
SPECIES, CHER'SIS ("pen-marked").

The full-fed, or nearly full-fed, caterpillars of this species are found very often on or near ash saplings, privet, or lilac, and crawling away from taller ash-trees when ready to burrow for pupation. They are large white-green crawlers, with a green or a bluish horn tipped with pink or all bluish, and white obliques edged above with dark green. Their heads have yellowish face-lines. Most of them prove to have been stung and are disappointments, so it was a great satisfaction to us when, one dull morning, we saw a robin fly from the fringe-tree on the lawn with a great green wriggler in his bill. The writhing of a large caterpillar makes it a heavy load for a robin, and this one wriggled well. The robin came down on the grass, dropped the caterpillar, and prepared to peck it into quietness; but we were too quick for him, and he flew from us, leaving the crawler for our examination. It was a fine *chersis*, not injured by its capture, and we put it away with a feeling of thanks to the robin, and then searched the fringe-tree. This was still better, for we found seven *chersis* larvæ of various sizes, and two eggs. It did seem to us a little hard that we

Sphinx chersis.

should profit by the information given us by the robin when it was so much to his disadvantage, but we knew that he could have access to other fringe-trees in our neighbors' grounds, and we thought of the many pea-pods he had opened, the peas he had eaten, and the cherries and early pears he had spoiled by pecking holes in their best sides, and hardened our hearts. It seemed fair that we should profit by his food, since he profited by ours.

We searched that fringe-tree daily the rest of the season, into October, and every few days we found eggs, or caterpillars from eggs laid too high on the tree for us to see them. Almost every caterpillar was stung, we found later, but from the eggs we reared perfect larvæ, pupæ, and moths.

The next year we began our search the first of July, and found eggs just ready to hatch. For three years we found eggs and larvæ on that tree from early July until late September, the last caterpillars feeding until late in October. During this time there was not a week when we failed to find eggs, showing that the moths were flying constantly from June till late September, and that if there are two broods they overlap, having no interval.

The eggs were ovoid, bright green, and always on the under side of the leaves, one on a leaf. We marked leaves as having no eggs on them, and then examined them daily until we found eggs. This gave us the date of egg-laying and the length of the egg-period. The eggs turned almost white before hatching, and the egg-period was six days in some instances, seven in others.

The hatchlings were cream-white, with brownish horns growing dark brown at tip and ending in two setæ. After eating, the caterpillars were green, except the head and the thoracic and anal segments, which were yellowish. They wandered a long time before settling on a leaf to feed, and did not eat their shells. Some of them did not eat at all for thirty-six hours, but drank eagerly. They all had a long, slender, glassy look after eating.

In a week they molted. The head was less round, more green, rough with yellow-white granules, and had yellow face-lines. The body was whitish green, with yellow-white granules, obliques, and subdorsal lines. The legs were green with pink tips, the props green, the anal plate was edged with yellow-white granules. The caudal horn was long, slender, rough, and pink.

In four days they molted again. The head was very yellow-green, triangular, with bright yellow granules and face-lines. The body was whiter green, rough with white granules. There were wide white subdorsal lines from head to horn, narrow white substigmatal lines on the thoracic segments, and yellow-white obliques. The legs were green with red tips, the props green, the anal plate was edged with yellow-white. The horn was red, darkest at tip, with black spines. It was held horizontal, making a line with the dorsum. Two days later the subdorsal lines could be seen on the thoracic segments only; the obliques were edged above with deep green; the horn was red in front, green behind, and yellow at the sides from the last pair of obliques. It was rough and held sometimes upright, sometimes horizontal.

The third molt came four days later. The only changes were dots, instead of granules, on the body, and green all over the horn, with black spines on its front. The horn was held nearly horizontal.

Six days later the fourth molt took place. The head was almost triangular, slightly bilobed at the apex, and green, with faint white dots and yellow face-lines. The thoracic segments were bright green, rough with white granules. The abdominal segments were bright green on the sides and ventor, almost white on the dorsum, with white dots. The obliques were yellow-white, edged above with deep blue-green. The horn was long, stout, rough, curving backward, sometimes green, sometimes bluish, sometimes bluish with a pink tip, occasionally pinkish; and two or three had the horns green, with blue at the base in front. The legs were reddish, the props green dotted with white, and the anal plate was very yellow-green, edged with still yellower. The spiracles were dark, surrounded by a yellowish line, and conspicuous.

As they grew older the thoracic segments were smoother, until at last the granules were hardly more than dots. The caterpillars ate ravenously after this molt, and grew to a length of four inches. They ate for four days, then grew moist and lay on the tin, pupating four days later. Usually they need no earth in the tin, but one or two exuded so much fluid that we put them on a little earth.

Unlike all other sphingid larvæ we have watched in pupation, *chersis* rests on the venter through all the quiet time of preparation for casting the larva-skin. The first sign of readiness to cast the skin was a somewhat distended look about the abdominal segments. The thoracic segments were bent forward and downward, so that the flat "face" of the head lay on the ground. Two brown dashes appeared on the third segment, one on each side of the dorsal line, and on the front edge of each side of the eighth, ninth, and tenth segments, near the spiracles, appeared a similar but paler dash. The body was constricted between the abdominal segments. The head, body, and horn were of a pale, dirty green, and all the markings of the caterpillar had vanished, the skin looking dry and detached between the abdominal segments. At intervals shivers ran through the body, as if it felt a sharp and sudden pain.

Next there appeared on the dorsum of each abdominal segment a brown band, which, when examined with a lens, was made up of small brown punctures set close together.

Next the skin wrinkled on the eighth and ninth segments, still more on the tenth, and grew whiter between them. The seventh, eighth, ninth, and tenth segments became distended still more, and the skin grew white on the sides like a slight water-blister.

At this point the first five segments were bent to one side a little. The skin grew more wrinkled and detached-looking, though no perceptible motion of the pupa wrinkled it. A white dorsal line appeared on the first segment and extended to the dashes on the third, though not immediately. Three hours had passed while the larva was watched, if it can be called a larva, since really it was the pupa in the larva-skin.

Sphinx chersis.

The rest of the process until the pupa was free occupied thirty-one minutes.

The skin grew more wrinkled on the anal end, and stretched taut over the abdominal segments, while the lower part of the body began to contract and expand in such wise as to move up toward the third segment, and with such force that the skin split before and between the brown dashes on that segment, then parted as far as the head. At this point the creature turned over on its back.

The third segment was pushed out first, then the second, then the mask was split, and the first segment came out, while the head was loosened from the old skin, and first the antennæ, then the tongue-case, then the legs appeared separate and free from the body; but as the head was pulled out they fell into place on the thorax, and lay close to it and to each other. This explains the position of the caterpillar's head in the beginning. The appendages must lie flat on the thorax for safety and compactness, and the drawing backward of the head in freeing itself from the larva-skin causes them to fall into their places. It is one of the most beautiful processes of adaptation we have ever seen, although it fails now and then, when the pupa either dies or gives an imperfect moth.

The rest of the pupation was very rapid. The segments in the larva-skin contracted while those without expanded, thus pushing the skin down. Each segment, as it emerged, expanded in its turn, and the pushing was almost continuous until the skin dropped off the anal end of the soft, green, shapeless — or nearly so — pupa.

The pupa lay quiet for a few moments, then began to writhe at the anal end, and to contract there until this segment was in pupa shape.

The tongue-case consisted of two broad tubes, more like flaps than tubes. They lay with their tips on the thorax, about one third of the distance down the wing-covers, and separate. The head and first two segments were still bent forward, though not as much as before pupation. The head began to draw back very slowly, as did the thoracic segments, and very slowly the tongue-case and wing-covers lengthened, until, two hours later, they were of the normal length and the whole pupa had settled into normal shape and had begun to turn brown. Almost two days were needed for the color to become chestnut-brown, the wings being the last part to lose their clear green color. When wholly developed into normal pupæ they were deep chestnut-brown.

The pupæ were long and rather slender, with a short tongue-case appressed to the thorax in most instances, but in some raised a little near the head. The largest pupæ measured two and a half inches in length, the smallest one and seven eighths inches.

Chersis larvæ are very quiet and not easily excited or disturbed, but they are subject to some diseases which seem to affect them most just as we think we have them almost full fed. We have never been able to find any cause for these diseases, but we have lost some fine crawlers by them.

Sometimes a hatchling seems to find the leaf too tough for its mandibles, but if a bit of the margin is torn away the little caterpillar will begin on the torn edge and soon eat as well as any of the brood. Usually they eat small holes through the middle of the upper part of the leaf first, then attack the margin. Holes near the tips of leaves have guided us to many small *chersis* larvæ.

The moths are large and strong. They are gray, with marks of white and black, especially the black dashes on the fore wings, which give the name of the " pen-marked sphinx " by which the moths are known. The coloring is very clear, and the moths have a clean-cut, elegant appearance. With one exception, ours have not emerged until the following summer. In the very hot summer of 1901 one female moth emerged in August. They fly after dark, and have long tongues, feeding at deep flowers. Their range is wide, covering the country from ocean to ocean, and from Canada to Georgia, according to Mr. Beutenmüller, who finds them double-brooded near New York.

DOLBA HYLÆUS

GENUS,   DOL′BA.
SPECIES,   HYLÆ′US (a centaur. There is no appropriateness).

It was a joyful day for us when one of the children brought us "a gray little moth, not a bit pretty. Perhaps you don't want it." We did want it, and gladly paid the price offered for "anything we want very much," for no description of *Dolba hylæus'* early stages had been published, and this was an egg-layer.

The eggs were pale green, oval, and grew yellowish five days after they were laid, hatching on the seventh day.

The caterpillars were less than a quarter of an inch long, green, with black caudal horns nearly as long as their bodies. They would eat nothing but inkberry, *Prinos glabra,* and after feeding they grew pinkish, especially near the head and horn. They spun threads as they crawled, and some died from being entangled in these threads, so we separated the rest, having only one or two in a box.

They fed for a week before molting, then molted, ate all their cast skins, and looked just as they did before, only longer, but in a day or two they showed faint white subdorsal lines from head to horn. The horn was black, the segment at its base whitish green.

158

Dolba hylæus.

The second molt was a week after the first. This time they had seven pale yellow-white obliques, the last being whiter and wider than the others and extending up the horn. There was a dark dorsal line from head to horn, and the horn was browner.

The third molt, six days later, made them an inch long, a trifle longer when they crawled. The head was green, the body pale green on the dorsum with a dark green dorsal line, and deeper green elsewhere, with a yellow lateral line broken by the yellow obliques, which were edged above with dark green. The horn was long, sharp, and rough, green at the base, almost black elsewhere. The legs and props were green. The body was granulated with yellow, and most densely on the thoracic segments. In this stage the yellow horizontal lateral line disappeared from the abdominal segments after two days. The last pair of obliques became edged above with blue-black, and the head gained blue-black granules. The legs became red-brown at the tips. One caterpillar showed his individuality by having an olive-green horn, very pale at the tip.

Five days later the fourth molt occurred. The head was round, green, granulated. The body was green, and granulated with yellow on the thoracic segments, venter, and anal shield. The dorsum was very white-green, with a deep green dorsal line. There were no yellow lateral lines. The obliques were whiter, edged above with dark green, then a faint blue-black line, the last one whiter, wider, and having a marked blue-black line. The spiracles were blue-black encircled with white, inconspicuous even now. The caudal horn was green at base, blackish green on the front and lighter behind, slightly rough, pointed, long, and slender. The legs were green at base, then yellow, and had blue-black tips. The props were green, and the anal shield was edged with yellow-green. The crawlers ate more now, but were dainty and seldom ate the whole of a leaf, eating part and then leaving it for another. They were never voracious like *celeus* or *lineata*, and in all their ways belonged to the aristocracy, if we may think of caterpillars as aristocratic.

For six days they ate and grew, but showed no signs of pupating, and surprised us by molting for the fifth time. This time they changed much. The head was blue-green, with small dark warts or tubercles, and had a line of blue-purple on the edge so far back as to be hidden by the first segment when at rest. The body was yellow-green, very white-green on the dorsum. The thoracic segments and venter were granulated with white. The obliques were bright pink, shading into yellow on the dorsum, and edged above with deep green. The last pair were white instead of yellow, and continued up the sides of the horn as white granules. The horn was blue-green in front and behind, the anal plate lightly edged with yellow. The dorsal line was very blue-green, edged on each side with white. The legs were green, ringed with yellow, and had blue-black tips. The props were green. The caterpillars measured an inch and a half in length and were rather slender.

Two days later the dark green edges of the obliques and the green of the horn changed to a purple-black, showing more purple beneath the horn.

Five days after this change the yellow granules became faint dots, and the obliques next the head grew very faint, being yellow edged with green, while all the others were bright pink edged with deep blue-purple. The horn was of this same deep blue-purple, except the green base. This purple is exactly the color of ripe inkberries. The spiracles were now dark in ovals of white edged with a faint blue-purple line, and were small, merged in the pink obliques on six segments, but conspicuous on the others.

The caterpillars fed for fifteen days after the fifth molt, and grew to a length of two and a half inches. Then they stopped eating and lay quiet on the tin. Out of doors they go into the ground.

Eight days later the pupæ cast the caterpillar-skin, having passed from the egg to the pupa in fifty-four days, a long life for sphingid larvæ. Some of the pupæ were a little over an inch and a quarter long, the average being just about an inch and a quarter, with a short tongue-case appressed to the thorax. The color was bright brown.

Few, even among sphingid larvæ, are as pretty and dainty-looking as *Dolba hylæus*, and the clean, clear green of the inkberry sets them off and adds to the daintiness. They are delicate caterpillars and must be carefully treated, having enough food supplied to enable them to go from one leaf to another without eating all of any leaf.

We cannot hear of any place where they are really common, but their range is wide — "from Canada to Florida, and west to Iowa," Mr. Beutenmüller says.

11

We have found but few *hylæus* caterpillars, and ink-berry and *Prinos* of the other species were the only food-plants they would eat. Probably others will be discovered some day, though the coloring of the cater-pillars fits them for the inkberry better than for any other plant.

Like most sphingid caterpillars, when half and full grown they rest on the twig under the leaves. Seen from above they are inconspicuous, because the venter and sides, which are uppermost, are of just the color of the upper surface of the leaves. When the twig is turned over they are equally inconspicuous, because the dorsum is of just the white-green of the under side of the leaves, while the outline of the caterpillar is broken by blue-purple like the berries and pink like the buds.

The moths are rust-brown, black, and white, the brown varying much in shade, being sometimes pale ocher-brown, sometimes pale chestnut-brown, at others very red-brown. The fore wings have a rich, velvety look, are crossed by wavy lines of black and white, and have a distinct discal dot on each. The hind wings are smoky white at base, almost black at the outer margin, and crossed by a black band, or by two black bands, more or less distinct. The thorax is brown mottled with black, the abdomen brown, with black and white spots and bars, the ventral surface being white.

The under side of the wings is coffee-brown, with darker brown margin and wavy lines of darker brown and white. The antennæ are ciliate in the male, sim-

ple in the female.   The legs are brown, so ringed with
white as to look speckled.

The redder moths are very pretty, and once seen
can never be mistaken for any others.   There is a peculiar richness in their coloring and the denseness of
their scales.

CERATOMIA AMYNTOR

GENUS, CERATO'MIA ("horned shoulders").
SPECIES, AMYN'TOR (named for the king of the Dolopians).

When we were little girls and had not outgrown our nurse's horror of creeping things, we used to be much disturbed by "great, big, horny caterpillars" which came down from the elms between which our swing hung, and crawled about very fast, sometimes in numbers which drove us away from the swing for a day or two in August or September. Now we think of each of those fine crawlers as a lost chance, and do not thank our nurse for the silly fear she gave us.

Such caterpillars are the "elm-tree sphinx," and we have never found them on any other tree, though they are said to feed on linden and white birch as well. They feed high up on the tree, and the usual way of obtaining them is to catch them when they come down to go into the ground, though One of Us once found five on an elm sapling. We had had many full-grown larvæ of this kind, but our first set of eggs has a story. An English entomologist wrote to ask if we could send him eggs of *amyntor*, and a few days later, in July, One of Us was walking along a street in a town — not the country — when she saw on a stone slab at some distance a triangular projection which

164

suggested a possible moth. Crossing the street, she found not only a moth, but an *amyntor* female, and succeeded in boxing it without injury. This is the kind of chance which makes caterpillar- and moth-hunting so exciting. It was mere chance that One of Us walked in that direction, and that the moth had stayed until nearly noon on a milestone under an electric light in a much-traveled street. It was not wholly chance that she spied the moth, because entomologists have a way of seeing most things.

Amyntor certainly fulfilled our wildest hopes. She laid one hundred and forty eggs in three nights, and there were enough for the English entomologist and for us, so we kept about a third of them with a clear conscience. They were very pale apple-green, showing the larva later as a white line. They hatched in six days.

The young caterpillars were three sixteenths of an inch long, and almost white until they had eaten, when they grew green all over,— but a very pale green,— with short, sparse setæ. On the dorsum of the second and third segments were two folds of skin, or tiny pits with an edge raised a little — the beginning of the thoracic horns. When disturbed the caterpillars dropped from the leaf by threads which they spun. The first day they ate nothing, not even their shells, but they drank water eagerly, and the next day they ate holes through elm-leaves. On the third day they showed white subdorsal lines from the head to the horn, which was still almost white. They showed also a broken white dorsal line on the abdominal segments, and the four thoracic horns appeared as slight excrescences in place of the pits.

They molted when five days old, coming out a little over half an inch long, and rough with yellow granules. The head was small and blue-green, the body yellow-green, with short setæ, as in the last stage. The horn was pale green with dark gray spines, and the other marks were like those of the last stage.

Four years later the Other of Us found a moth, early in the morning, on an elm trunk, and the larvæ from its eggs differed a little in this stage from our first ones. They were glassy green with yellow-white granules, had dorsal, lateral, and oblique lines of white granules, and a collar of these on the first segment. The horn was pinkish, with black thorns. The sub-dorsal line was confined to the thoracic segments. Both broods had the thoracic horns well developed.

Four days later the first brood molted. The second brood was six days between these molts. The head was somewhat triangular, bilobed, green, granulated, and had face-lines of yellow granules. The body was green, with transverse rows of yellow-white granules, not a bright yellow. The collar on the first segment was of sharp thorn-like granules, and the dorsal line was a crest of sharp thorns, the obliques being of the same thorn-like granules. The second and third segments had a row of thorns from the horns backward. The obliques reached to the dorsal line, and with that made an excellent imitation of the midrib and veins of the back of an elm-leaf, being exactly of its color. The caudal horn was green, granulated with yellow-white on the sides, and with black elsewhere. The spiracles were yellow, with a dark ring. The legs and props were green; the anal plate had a smooth yellow edge.

In six days they molted for the third time, and were unchanged, except that they had grown to a length of one and a quarter inches. Four came out a dirty greenish brown, with light brown marks.

The first brood molted in seven days, the second in four, this time. They were two inches long, and as before, except that some were very white-green, some very blue-green, some yellow-green, and others brown of various shades. All the brown ones had the lines and obliques of a pink-brown, the thorns on the thoracic horns yellow, and the anal plate and props of a dark, soft, velvet brown. Their heads were dark brown with lighter face-lines, and their legs and props were brown. One was of green overshot with brown.

When full grown they measured three and a half inches in length, and exactly resembled green or brown elm-leaves curled together lengthwise, as elm-leaves often do curl. So perfect was the resemblance that several persons who asked to see them put their hands on the crawlers, expecting to unfold leaves.

The first brood ate ravenously for five days, the second for seven; then the green caterpillars grew pink on their backs, the brown ones redder, and all stopped eating and began crawling.

Amyntor larvæ exude so much fluid in pupating that they do better on a little earth, though we have had fine pupæ without it. Out of doors they go into the ground to transform.

It was just a week before the pupæ came from the larva-skins. They were an inch and three quarters long, not stout, but very solid-feeling. They were of a dark red-brown, showing no tongue-case, and had on each side of the dorsum, behind the thorax, an open crescent. They were very active, wriggling and rolling when their box was opened.

One peculiarity the larvæ had just before pupation, when they were shrunken and moist: they gave out a delicious fragrance, like very sweet mignonette, we thought. One of our visitors thought it more like orris.

We have found no stung specimens of *amyntor*, as far as our records show or our memories go, but the caterpillars sometimes die from a disease which seems to liquefy them internally and leave a limp, empty skin.

They are rather common where elms are found, from Canada to Virginia, and west as far as Missouri and Iowa. They are not considered to be double-brooded and seem to straggle along, the moths beginning to fly in June and the latest caterpillars crawling down to the ground in October, in New England.

Moths may be found early in the morning on the west side of elm trunks, where daylight has overtaken them. They may be caught about electric lights and at bait or flowers. They fly rather late. They are brown,— coffee-brown and clay-brown,— with black dashes, and white about the head, collar, and thorax. The abdomen is clay-brown, with three black stripes.

It is safe to say that the caterpillars have frightened more persons than any other harmless crawler except *polyphemus*, since these two are more often found crawling on sidewalks when ready to pupate. Yet their thorny horns are entirely harmless and do not even give out an urticating fluid.

Some entomologists have found *amyntor* larvæ on linden and white birch, as well as on elm.

Ceratomia amyntor.

Ceratomia undulosa.

CERATOMIA UNDULOSA

GENUS,   CERATO'MIA.
SPECIES,   UNDULO'SA ("wavy").

Eggs of these moths may be found on ash, lilac, and privet. In our experience the caterpillars are more common on ash and rather high on the tree, often too high to reach with an umbrella or a weighted string. The Other of Us has been known to sit down on the roadside and wait for a high-seated wagon to come along, and then ask the driver to reach for her the twigs with *undulosa* larvæ on them. The farmers are always very kind about doing this, though they want to know exactly why we wish the crawlers and what we mean to do with them.

The eggs were pale green, nearly globular, and hatched after eight days.

The hatchlings were pale greenish yellow, with horns more or less brown, long, and pointing backward. Food gave a greener color to the caterpillars.

After five days they molted, the head being pale green, with whitish granulation and face-lines. The body was of a little darker green, with a pale subdorsal line and white obliques.

The second molt followed in four days, and the caterpillars were very active after this change. They

169

were very slender in proportion to their length. When at rest they stood on their anal props and reared their bodies in the air, curving them somewhat like a question-mark reversed (⸮). They were of just the color of the under side of the ash-leaves. The head was large, pointed, and had whitish face-lines. The sub-dorsal line was confined to the first three segments. The last pair of obliques were yellow. The body was blue-green on the dorsum, yellow-green on the sides, and blue-green on the venter, the division being quite distinct. The horn was quite long, straight, pointed backward, pink, and covered with darker spines.

Four days later they molted for the third time. The head was green, somewhat triangular, with heavy white face-lines, granulated. The thoracic segments were covered with white granules, the anal segment having dark ones. The obliques were light yellow, edged above with dark green, the last pair growing very white. The horn was pinkish, with dark granules at the tip and on the front and back, and light ones on the sides. The legs were green, with pink tips. The spiracles were dull red, with a white dot at each end.

The fourth molt was nine days later. The head was triangular, large, and darker than the blue-green body, and had white face-lines, pinkish near the mouth. Both head and body were smooth now. The skin seemed to be in folds on the body. The obliques were white, the legs and props as before. The horn was pink and rough. The spiracles were dull red, with a yellow line down the middle.

The caterpillars fed for ten days after this molt, then turned lead-colored and stopped eating. The pupæ cast the larva-skin on the fourth day, and were dark chestnut-brown, with no raised tongue-case.

We have not found any larvæ before August, but the moths are double-brooded farther south. They are not uncommon, and range from Canada to Georgia, and from the Atlantic coast to Iowa.

The caterpillars are often mistaken for *chersis*, one entomologist telling us that he never could distinguish them until they pupated. Then he know of which species they were, because *chersis* has a tongue-case detached from the body, while *undulosa's* is level with the wing-covers.

The moths have brownish-gray wings with white and black marks, and a distinct white discal dot on each fore wing. The hind wings have three blackish bands not very clearly defined. The abdomen has large black spots on each side and a black dorsal line. The coloring varies much with different specimens, some having almost no brownish scales, others being very much whiter than the typical *undulosa*. The antennæ are simple in the female, but biciliate in the male.

The moths fly after dark and usually fly high, laying their eggs on the leaves of upper branches, though occasionally they may be found on saplings. The moths fly about electric lights and have not as swift flight as *chersis* or *lineata*.

The caterpillars crawl down the trunks of the trees to burrow in the ground for pupation, and often crawl long distances before the impulse to burrow comes to them. They are to be found on the sidewalks in the autumn, or crawling along country roads, at any time of day. On such occasions many fall victims to robins, which dance around them as if trying to choose the best spot for a peck, then seize them and carry them off a little way before killing them.

Several parasitic flies sting the caterpillars, sometimes when the larvæ are so small that they die, covered with cocoons, before the fourth molt.

X

SUBFAMILY SMERINTHINÆ

THIS subfamily is named from the fact that the antennæ are like cords or threads.

The moths have short tongues, and must therefore feed at shallow flowers. Most of them have the fore wings notched or scalloped. The caterpillars are rough-skinned, or granulated.

TRIPTOGON MODESTA

GENUS, TRIP'TOGON.
SPECIES, MODES'TA ("modest").

Our egg-layer of this species was found under an electric light, near a large "balm-of-Gilead" poplar. She was so battered and rubbed, and lacked so much more of her wings than was left, that we were not sure of her identity, though we hoped that she might prove to be *modesta*. She laid a hundred and thirty-two eggs in three nights, and then died. She began egg-laying before three o'clock in the afternoon each day, leading us to suppose that these moths fly early as well as late.

The eggs were ovoid, and greenish gray with a pearly luster. They were laid near each other in irregular groups, probably because the moth's wings were so broken that she could not fly to oviposit, but could only crawl around the box.

The eggs looked greener by night and gray by day, were finely shagreened, and turned heliotrope-color on the second day, then, five days later, greener, showing the larvæ curled inside. They hatched on the seventh day, and the young caterpillars showed why the eggs turned green at last, for they were dark green, the dorsum looking undershot with black, except the last two segments, which were very pale green, as was the head. All were rough. There was a pale yellow sub-dorsal line from the head to the tip of the anal props, and there were faint, pale green obliques, rougher than the body. The anal props had a projection in the rear, like the train of a dress. The props were pale green, the legs pale green with red tips, and the horn was bright carmine, short, straight, and very per-pendicular — rough also.

The little caterpillars were very active, began feed-ing very soon, and some ate all of their egg-shell, while others ate only enough to make their way out. They rested "standing on their hind legs," as one of the children said, holding the midrib of a leaf with the anal props, and raising the rest of the body in the air, not quite vertically.

They molted in four days, were nearly twice as long as before, and had heads not quite triangular in shape and bifid at the apex, or looking so because the apex ended in two large yellow granules. The whole head was studded with yellow granules and had yellow face-lines. The body was dark green, with subdorsals and obliques of bright yellow granules, the obliques meeting on the dorsal line. The first segment was crested with yellow granules, and on the dorsum of the second and third segments there was a transverse band of yellow granules from one subdorsal line to the other, on the rear edge of each segment. The venter was blue-green, with whiter granules; the anal plate was edged with yellow granules. The legs were red, and the props blue-green with white granules. The horn was yellow, with a bright carmine spot at the base in front, and rough with red granules. They ate all their skins except the horns and masks.

In three days they molted again, and were much as before, except that the subdorsals were fainter, the face-lines yellower and broader, and the very short horn was pinkish yellow, with a brown double dot at the base in front; there was a dark brown spot at the tip of each anal prop and on each leg. The yellow granules of the transverse lines on the thorax were almost spikes, like those of the dorsal line of *amyntor*. Three days later the legs had become yellow, with red tips, and the crest on the first segment was hardly noticeable.

The striking points of the larvæ were the deep, velvety-green color, the yellow bands of granules on the second and third segments, and the last pair of broad yellow obliques, coloring the short horn.

The third molt followed the second in four days. The caterpillars were now not an inch long. The head was more triangular, pale green, with pale yellow granules and yellow face-lines meeting at the apex of the head. The first segment was pale green, granulated, with no noticeable crest of granules. The rest of the body was deep moss-green, densely set with tiny yellow granules, except the anal segment, which was bright yellow-green, with very small yellow granules, and the anal plate was edged with yellow granules, covered with glassy-green ones, and had a dark red-brown spot at the tip. The second and third segments had conspicuous crests of yellow spikes, and the very narrow obliques were of yellow granules, the last pair being broader and yellower. The abdominal segments

had a broken substigmatal line of yellow granules. The legs were yellow, with a dark brown spot and red tips, the props green, granulated with yellow. The anal props had a dark brown spot at the tip. The horn was very short, rough, and pale yellow. The spiracles were red. The granules in this molt suggested *amyntor*. Three days later the larvæ lost the rich moss-green color and became blue-green, while the very yellow marks were whiter. The caterpillars now ate more and were less active.

The fourth molt followed the third in six days. The caterpillars were a little more than an inch and a half long, and largest at the anal end, tapering to the head. The head was very white-green on the sides, with white dots, while the front was of a peculiar pink-purple color, with pink face-lines. The first segment of the body was very white-green, the anal segment was very yellow-green, those between were very blue-green, and all were dotted with white. On each side of the third, fourth, and fifth segments of some was a red-purple spot on the subdorsal line, suggesting *myops*. Others had from three to ten red-purple spots on each side. The subdorsal line was no longer visible. The obliques were of small white granules, except the last pair, which were wider, rougher, and pinkish. The crests on the thoracic segments were much lessened, hardly noticeable. The mouth-parts, legs, and tips of the props were pink-purple, and the anal props had a band of deep red-purple. The spiracles were red-purple in pink-purple spots. The caudal horn was very short, very slender, white, and rough. The anal plate was heart-shaped, swelling, with dark red-purple tip. The

12

caterpillars were now very pretty, and ate more than at first, though they were never as hungry as *celeus.* In different stages they suggested the caterpillars of *H. thysbe, C. amyntor,* and *P. myops,* and were very interesting.

The balm-of-Gilead gives out a fragrance so aromatic that the boxes were always pleasant to open, and the caterpillars themselves were dainty and beautiful; they were over three inches long at last.

They stopped eating five days after the fourth molt, and six days later the pupæ molted the larva-skin.

The pupæ were about two inches long, dark brown, almost black, shagreened, and very stout. No tongue-case was visible. They were very quiet pupæ, although in fine condition.

The moths emerged the following summer. They are beautiful with shades of gray and mouse-color, and the hind wings have red or pink-red through the middle, and a bluish patch at the anal angle. The head, thorax, and abdomen are of bluer gray than the wings, which vary much in tint and marking, being sometimes of almost uniform brown, sometimes having olive, sometimes bluish reflections. The pink-red of the hind wings is of the same class of color as that of *P. geminatus* and *P. excæcatus,* and the under side of the fore wings has a patch of this color.

In the West the moths are much paler than in the East and North, and are called (variety) *occidentalis.*

Modesta is a more Northern than Southern species, but "is found from the Atlantic to the Pacific." It is thought to be double-brooded, but our August pupæ gave no moths until the following summer.

Smerinthus geminatus.

SMERINTHUS GEMINATUS

GENUS, SMERIN'THUS (a cord — antennæ like cords).
SPECIES, GEMINA'TUS (twin — the eye-spots are double).

The first time we encountered *geminatus* was a chance lost. We found a white birch with many rather large, ovoid green eggs laid singly on the under side of the leaves. In a few days the eggs hatched, and as the little caterpillars grew and changed they seemed alike, except that some were bluer-green than others — a difference not unusual in *excœcatus*, which we had reared and thought we had again found. When the moths emerged the next summer, part proved *geminatus*, and we were much disgusted that we had not recognized the larvæ and kept their record. Even now, however, we should not feel sure of distinguishing *geminatus* from *excœcatus* unless we had eggs from a moth we had seen, or which had been seen by some one who knew. The books give *geminatus* a blue or violet caudal horn and *excœcatus* a green or bluish one, but we have seen both in one brood of the latter, and cannot consider this difference in color a sure test; moreover, some *geminatus* larvæ have pink horns.

Our next experience was with eggs found on poplar, and we kept a record of the crawlers, whose egg-stage is doubtless about as long as that of *excœcatus* — about seven days.

The hatchlings were pale green, granulated, and unmarked. Their caudal horns were dark brown and
rough; in another brood were gray or red at first,
turning black in a few hours. The horns were straight,
long, and slender. The heads were wider at the bottom
than at the top, but not really triangular, as they became in later stages.

The caterpillars began to eat poplar at once, standing on the edge of a leaf and eating through the whole
leaf, cutting curves out of the margin, instead of eating
only the parenchyma, as do many young larvæ. They
did not eat the egg-shells. On the second day pale
yellow subdorsal and oblique lines showed faintly, the
former extending from head to horn and crossed by
the obliques. Faint white granules also appeared, becoming clearer on the third day.

On the fifth day the caterpillars molted, having triangular, white-green heads rough with white granules,
yellowish face-lines, and two yellowish granules at the
apex. Their bodies were very pale green, with yellow-
white granules and yellow-white subdorsal lines, widest
on the thoracic segments, crossed by the yellow-white
obliques, the last pair of which was widest and yel-
lowest. The legs were green with pink tips, the props
green, and the anal props were prolonged at the lower
end in the rear, like those of *modesta*. The horns were
short, rough, almost black in front and rear, but yellow-
white on the sides from the last pair of obliques. All
the lines were formed of granules, the larger ones being
sharp. The caterpillars ate their skins, except the
horny masks.

In four days they molted again, being much as be-

fore, though the subdorsal line was confined to the
thoracic segments, the horn was green with a pinkish
tip, and the spiracles now were visible, having a red
line at each side.

Six days later they molted for the third time, coming out blue-green, with yellow-white subdorsal and
oblique lines, and whitish granules. The first pair of
obliques was very faint below the subdorsal line, and
the sixth pair hardly showed. The spiracles were
white, with a blue-black line at each side. Some had
blue horns, rough with blue and white granules. Others
had pink horns with pink granules. Part of the larvæ
surprised us by making ready to pupate eight days
later, while the others were molting for the fourth
time.

After the fourth molt about half of the caterpillars
had pink horns, the rest blue ones. All but one had
the last pair of obliques pink, and all lost the pink
before pupating. They were like the third molt in
other respects.

The pupæ formed three days after the caterpillars
stopped eating. They were stout, smooth, and chestnut-brown, and had no raised tongue-case.

Those caterpillars which pupated after the third
molt were twenty-six days in passing from egg to
pupa; the others were thirty-four days.

The moths are much more beautiful than *excœcatus,*
which they resemble somewhat. The head is gray,
the thorax gray with a patch of dark velvety brown.
The tongue is short. The fore wings are falcate and
slightly notched, violet-gray or gray in color, and
crossed by cyanic, or pale violet, and brown wavy

lines, with a marked discal dot, an apical brown spot edged with a white crescent, and two or three brown patches. The hind wings are rose-pink, with a putty-colored border, a double blue eye-spot encircled with black, and a brown patch at the anal angle. The abdomen is gray, with a deep brown tip; the legs are gray and brown, the palpi brown. The antennæ are almost white above, brown beneath, pectinate in the male and simple in the female.

The under side of the fore wings has a rose-colored patch, is browner than the upper side, and is crossed by brown and white wavy lines. The under side of the hind wings is browner still, crossed by wavy lines, and has a white dash. The moths vary much in the shades of coloring, but are never as brown as *excœcatus*. When first emerged they are sometimes almost violet, but grow grayer. The female is paler and less distinctly marked than the male. They fly in the evening and may be caught at light, or on white walls which catch distant light. We have taken them in hotel corridors between ten and eleven o'clock, and have found them, newly emerged, on tree-trunks in the morning.

The caterpillars may be found on willow, poplar, spiræa, hazel, birch, ash, oak, wild-cherry, apple, plum, elm, ironwood and hornbeam, according to the books. Poplar, spiræa, and white birch have been our best food-plants for them.

The caterpillars are very clean, are not delicate, and have no diseases as far as we know. Out of doors they are very often victims of parasitic flies, and there they burrow in the ground to pupate.

The species is not uncommon, though not as common as *excœcatus*, "from Canada to Virginia, and westward to Iowa," according to Mr. Beutenmüller. It is considered to be double-brooded, and may be so in more southern places, but ours — in Vermont and Massachusetts — have not emerged before the following summer, though they have pupated in late June or early July. Those pupating in September and October would naturally pass the winter as pupæ.

PAONIAS EXCŒCATUS

GENUS,   PAO'NIAS   ("obliged": no appropriateness).
SPECIES,   EXCŒCA'TUS ("blind-eyed" — probably an allusion to the eye-spots).

We begin to think that we might rear *excœcatus* every year and have a different tale to tell each time. It is a common species, the caterpillars being found on willow, cherry,— both wild and cultivated,— white birch, poplar, oak, apple, pear, plum, rose, spiræa, hazel, hornbeam, ironwood, ash, raspberry, wistaria, *Pyrus japonica*, and probably on other trees and shrubs. Its range is all through Canada and the eastern United States. It is one of the first sphingid caterpillars which beginners find, and if they rear many broods of *excœcatus* they will become hardened to surprises.

The moths fly to lights and are often found resting on the side of the house or under the piazza-roof in the morning. We have found them on tree-trunks out of the sunlight as late as noon, and newly emerged moths at about eight o'clock in the morning, already spread and nearly dry enough to fly, yet they are night-fliers.

All the eggs we have seen have been ovoid, bright green, and shining, and have turned whiter before hatching. This seems the one fixed point in their history.

Paonias excœcatus (a small specimen).

One brood had an egg-period of ten days; another of eight; another of seven.

One brood had the molts follow in five, five, seven, eight days; another in four, four, seven, five days; a third in seven, five, seven, seven days.

One brood fed, after the last molt, for sixteen days, one for twelve, another for ten days. One brood was seven days in pupating, another five.

One set of hatchlings was pale green, granulated, unmarked, with a dark brown, rough horn; preferred *Pyrus japonica*. Another was green, granulated, with yellow obliques and a yellow lateral horizontal line on the thoracic segments; ate oak. A third brood was green, granulated with yellow, had yellow face-lines, yellow subdorsals from head to horn, and yellow obliques. Three of this brood had plain green horns, but the others had horns yellow at the base, then bright red, with a ring of yellow half-way to the tip. They fed on poplar. A fourth brood had smooth green heads, dotted with white. The bodies were rough and green, with faint white subdorsal and oblique lines. These had horns red at base and tip and pale green between. They preferred white birch.

None ate the egg-shells, and all were very active. When disturbed they reared on their anal props and angrily jerked their heads and thoracic segments over to one side, keeping the curled position until all cause of disturbance was removed. Their heads were round.

After the first molt the heads were shaped like apple-seeds with the point uppermost, and all the broods were like their first stage except one, which had a crest of yellow granules on the first segment, red tips to the legs, and the caudal horn green at the base, dark red next, yellowish in the middle, and red at the tip. This was the fourth brood.

After the second molt the first brood had yellow granules, yellow face-lines, and the anal shield edged with yellow. The horns were red at base and tip, yellow between. The third brood lost the subdorsals, except on the thoracic segments, and gained the crest of yellow granules on the first segment, and a double yellow granule on each side of the dorsal line of the second and third segments. The red on the horns was much less. The fourth brood gained bright yellow face-lines, a red spot on each leg, and a yellow edge to the anal shield, and had horns red and yellow, with no green. The last pair of obliques was broad, very yellow, and extended up the caudal horn.

At the third molt the second brood was unchanged, except that the horn was yellowish, and the last pair of obliques was wide and very yellow, extending up the horn. The third brood gained red tips to the legs and a yellow edge to the anal plate, and lost all red from the horn. The fourth brood was unchanged, except that the head was bilobed.

After the fourth molt all were unchanged except the fourth brood. These were now bright apple-green, rough with yellow granules. The subdorsals and obliques were of heavier granules, the last pair of obliques heaviest and extending up the rough green horn, while in some cases the subdorsals reached from head to horn, in others only from the head to the first abdominal segment. The legs were green ringed with yellow, and had red tips. The props were green; the anal shield was edged with yellow. The horns were green, with yellow granules.

We hear of *excœcatus* caterpillars with red spots, like *myops*, but we have never seen one. Nothing would surprise us. Among the caterpillars we have found there have been very yellow-green ones, very blue-green ones, and very white-green ones; and sometimes a blue-green one would come out yellow-green after a molt. They are very satisfactory crawlers to rear, because they are not delicate and almost none die. Those found out of doors, however, are very often stung. Their length, when full grown, varies from two to nearly three inches, and they are largest at the seventh, eighth, and ninth segments, tapering to the head, and being slightly smaller behind the tenth segment.

The favorite resting-position of the nearly grown larva is that shown by the illustration, and is characteristic of *geminatus* and *astylus* as well. *Myops* is quite as likely to rest parallel to the leaf or stem.

The very rough granules of the full-grown caterpillars are characteristic of the *Smerinthinæ*, though *myops* is said by some writers to be smooth. Ours have been rough. All have had setæ when young.

The pupa is dark brown, pitted on the thorax and abdomen, shows no tongue-case, and is from an inch and a half to nearly two inches long, and rather stout.

The moths are less beautiful than *geminatus*, being browner. They vary much in tint, some being fawn-colored, others deeper brown with wavy lines crossing the fore wings, which are notched on the outer edge more than those of *astylus, myops*, or *geminatus*. The hind wings are pink edged with brown of varying shades, or almost all pink suffused with fawn-color on the front edge. Each has an eye-spot of blue heavily bordered with black, the border widest below. The head, thorax, and abdomen are fawn-color, with a darker, bright brown stripe through the middle. Two or three specimens have had the fore wings suffused with pink, as if the color of the under side showed through.

The antennæ of the males are widely pectinate, those of the females simple. This is an easy means of distinguishing between them.

PAONIAS MYOPS

GENUS,   PAO'NIAS   ("obliged").
SPECIES, MY'OPS   ("purblind"—alluding to the eye-spots probably).

Myops is another joy to the beginner, because it is common and beautiful. We had one of our earliest experiences with it one beautiful afternoon as we walked up the Lane after a rainy day. It was about five o'clock, and as we passed a wild-cherry tree One of Us spied a moving caterpillar just starting to crawl up a bough whose tip touched the ground. She picked it up, gave it a spray of cherry, and then we looked at it. It was *myops* beyond a doubt, but with spots of a bright carmine instead of the "red-brown" of the books. While One of Us put away number one, the Other of Us found three or four more crawling along the same bough, which evidently served as a bridge from the ground to the tree. Another was found on the trunk, and then we examined the grass near the tree, with no result but very wet garments and hands. We went on up the Lane, and when we came back the Other of Us said, in clear sarcasm: "Now find us a few more *myops* traveling up that same branch." "Very well," said One of Us, who was very far-sighted. "Here's the first one!" and she picked off three more just where some of the earlier ones had been found.

189

In all the years since we have never found a *myops* on that tree, but we never pass it without a feeling that we may see another procession. We often find single caterpillars on hazel-bushes which grow in a clump near a big rock, and on wild-cherry trees, especially young trees and saplings.

The first eggs we had were sent us by a friend; the second lot we found on the under side of leaves, eight on one leaf. The eggs were ovoid and pale green, and soon showed a white line — the caterpillar. The egg-period was fifteen days in the first instance; in the second we had no means of knowing; a third brood hatched in seven days. The first lot hatched the last week in June, the second on the 28th of July, the third about the middle of July.

The caterpillars were pale yellow, becoming yellow-green after eating, and had short setæ all over, as do all young sphingid larvæ. The caudal horn was pinkish, rough, short, and thick. They ate nearly all of their shells, drank eagerly, and ate holes in the parenchyma of the wild-cherry leaves, leaving the fibers untouched. They fed on the under side of the leaves always, clasping a vein with their props; but after a day or two they crawled to the edge of the leaf and ate curves out of it. They always rested at some distance from the feeding-place. Their anal props had "trains" like those of *T. modesta*. In a day or two faint yellow lines appeared on the side of the thoracic segments, and faint yellow obliques.

The first molt occurred five days after hatching. The first brood was unchanged, until three days later, when faint red spots began to show.

The second brood had the heads, first and anal seg-

ments blue-green, sparsely granulated with yellow. The rest of the body was yellow-green, densely granulated with yellow. The head was shaped like an apple-seed, though broader at `the large end, and had two large yellow granules at the apex — also like *T. modesta.* The first segment had two shorter yellow granules on the dorsum. The caudal horn was longer, pinkish at the tip, and very rough. The legs and props were green as before. The oblique and horizontal lines were of yellow granules set close together. A day or two later the horns became bright carmine, except on the sides, up which the last obliques extended. The legs were red at the tip, and a few caterpillars had small bright red spots on the fifth segment, one on each side of the dorsum.

The second molt was five days later. The first brood now had all the yellow and red markings, and the second was as before, except for faint yellow face-lines, denser granulation, and more red spots, the number varying from two to twelve per caterpillar.

The first brood molted in six days, the second in four, this time. The yellow granules on the apex of the head had become reduced to dots. The face-lines were of yellow granules. The bodies were still granulated. The horns were pale red in front, yellow behind and at the sides, short, triangular, and rough. The spiracles were red. The legs had red tips. There were from two to forty-eight red patches on the body. Two crawlers had their horns blue-green with yellow sides, and no red. Several found on willow had blue horns with red sides, and forty-eight very red spots, the last pair of obliques being suffused with red also.

Two days later all the red disappeared from the

caudal horns, but some caterpillars gained red patches on the abdominal props. The anal shield was pointed and edged with yellow. Some caterpillars had a stigmatal as well as subdorsal row of red patches, others had stigmatal patches on one or two segments only. In three cases the red spots were surrounded by yellow.

In all these larvæ the red was bright carmine, but we have found many *myops* caterpillars with the dull red-brown which most of the books give as characteristic. We have had more with the bright than with the dull red, and more of both than of the unspotted ones, though we do find a plain green *myops* once in a while. All are about two inches long.

Mr. Beutenmüller finds *myops* smooth instead of granulated, but ours have all been rough, and we have reared scores of them.

The caterpillars varied in the length of the last stage; some stopped eating in six days after the fourth molt, some in four days, others in seven. The pupæ cast the larva-skin about five days after the larvæ stopped eating.

The pupa is deep purple-brown, not as stout as that of *excæcatus*, and usually shorter and smoother. The tongue-case is not raised. There are punctures on the thorax and abdomen.

The moths are lovely, having fore wings of rich, deep brown, with wavy lines of lilac, and two small yellow patches which sometimes lengthen into bands. The head and thorax are brown, yellowish in the middle. The hind wings are of a clear, soft yellow bordered with brown, and each has an eye-spot of blue encircled with black.

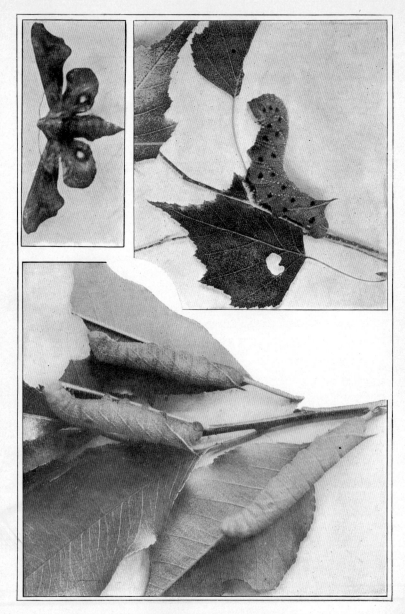

Paonias myops.

The antennæ of the male are strongly pectinate, of the female simple, so it is very easy to tell the egg-layer at a glance.

One peculiarity of the caterpillars did not come into our experience until after the foregoing account of them was type-written and ready for the printers. Then we had a large brood of *myops* from the egg, and we found that when ready to molt the crawlers did not fasten their anal props in any specially firm way, spun no mat of silk to fasten them in, as many caterpillars do, and molted just as well as if the old skin had been held fast for them to crawl out. More than this — the çaterpillars would leave the first place they had chosen for molting, and crawl even to other leaves or stems when molting was so far advanced that their masks were almost dropping off. This we had never before seen done by any caterpillar.

We watched the pupation of these *myops* and found that they crawled about the tin for hours, then became quiet, with the body rather shortened. After this each one curved to one side; then, after one or two days, it turned on its back, still curved and with the head bent forward over the thorax, and the feet drawn up under the mouth-parts. Thus it lay for hours, sometimes for a day, and imperceptibly the skin was pushed down, or the creature pushed itself up in it, so that the anal end was wrinkled and the abdominal segments looked distended. The lining of the spiracles appeared as the skin was pushed down; the skin burst on the third segment, and the pupa worked out, its antennæ, legs, etc., falling into place on the thorax as the head and thorax were drawn back and out. When the pupa

13

was free from the skin it began to settle into shape, contracting the abdomen and drawing the head and shoulders back into line with the rest of the body. From some hidden source a fluid oozed under the wing-cases, between them and the body, and often a little way beyond their edges. This fluid hardened into a thin membrane similar to that over the whole pupa, but not as firm and stiff. We had seen this membrane when moths emerged from their pupa-skins, but had not known how it was formed. Probably it exists in many, if not all, pupæ, but we have not examined more than five or six. All of these had the membrane. In some of the attacine pupæ it was very easy to see as the moths emerged.

Paonias astylus (showing eggs of parasitic fly).

PAONIAS ASTYLUS

GENUS,   PAO'NIAS.
SPECIES,   AS'TYLUS   (a seer among the centaurs: inappropriate).

This is the gem of the genus, and once seen the caterpillar cannot be forgotten, because of its beauty and
its wonderful resemblance to its food-plant.

We found our first one "up the Lane," a very favorite and productive walk of ours. It was late September, and the blueberry-bushes were gorgeous in red
and green, with the double-pointed leaf-buds formed
for the next year. On one of these bright bushes we
found — and we have never been able to tell who saw
it first — a caterpillar about two inches long and of
exactly the bright red and green of the leaves. No
jewel ever seemed more precious. We boxed it most
carefully and searched every bush in the neighborhood, but found no more then. Later we searched a
berry-pasture and found two more, one stung in many
places and useless to us.

No book gave us any help; for this was many years
ago, and less was known about the larvæ of many
moths than is known now.

We fed the two well, and they pupated finely; but
one filled with fungus, and the other gave parasitic
flies in the following spring, so we were no better off
for means of learning the name of the species. For

two or three years we had the same experience, but the next year gave us a moth or two, and we found out that it was *astylus*.

Later we found a moth which laid many eggs — fortunately, for *astylus* is a very delicate caterpillar, in our experience, and needs the most favorable conditions in order to thrive.

The eggs were almost globose, apple-green, and shining. They grew yellower, and before hatching the red caudal horns could be seen very plainly. The egg-period was eleven days with the first brood, ten with the second two years later. The eggs hatched in the evening, but fortunately we had provided blueberry-twigs, and could supply food at once.

The caterpillars were pale green, granulated, and had stout caudal horns, bifurcated at the tip, which was dark red, the horn growing lighter red to the base, and having a yellow band in the middle.

The first brood molted on the ninth, the second on the eighth day. The first brood was as before, except that the head was more pointed, yellow horizontal lateral lines appeared on the thoracic segments, and the legs were red. The second brood gained these marks and yellow obliques, a red dot at the apex of the now pointed head, and red patches on the subdorsal and stigmatal regions of some larvæ. Other larvæ lacked these patches. The red was bright carmine, and the patches were larger and more irregular in shape than those of *myops*.

The second molt followed in six days for both broods and brought no changes, except that the horns were less bifid, or had the two points shorter.

The third molt was eight days later for the first brood, seven for the second. The changes were slight, the horns being now still less bifid, each tip being a red granule or tubercle. Faint yellow obliques appeared, and the legs and props were all red at tip. The granulations of head and body were yellow.

The fourth molt followed in nine days for the first brood, in seven for the second. The head was green, with yellow granules, and had red face-lines. The green body was granulated with yellow, less roughly than before. The yellow obliques were clearer. A red horizontal line appeared on the side of the thoracic segments, and a faint yellow subdorsal line. The red spots and patches were brighter, larger, and more numerous than before, those near the dorsal line often suffusing the greater part of the segment as far down as the lateral line. The anal shield was edged and dotted with red. The legs and props had red tips. The spiracles were red. The caudal horn was rough, green at base, then red, then ringed with yellow, then darker red at tip. The tip ended in two red granules. The horn was straight, stout, and inclined forward. The red patches varied much, but the red increased on the larvæ as it did on the leaves, which were much redder now than five weeks earlier. In fact, we often wondered why we ever found one of these caterpillars, they so exactly matched the leaves on which they fed, and even their horns had two tiny tips, as had the next year's buds of the blueberry.

Some fed for seven days, some for nine, others for ten, after the fourth molt; then their colors grew dim, and they lay on the tins, pupating in from four to seven days. They ate much after the fourth molt, eating the common blueberry (*Vaccinium corymbosum*) and the dangleberry (*Gaylussacia frondosa*) equally well. Their length was about two inches, and they were largest at the eighth, ninth, and tenth segments.

The bifid caudal horn distinguishes *astylus* from all the *Smerinthinæ* we know.

The moth is rare in all stages, probably because it is so delicate and so often a victim to parasites. We have shown a stung larva in our illustration as being more often found than unstung ones.

The range of the species is not fully known. We are told that in New Jersey it has been found on willow, but blueberry, dangleberry, and *Andromeda ligustrina* are the only plants on which we have seen it, and on the last we have found but one specimen.

The pupa is dark brown, with concealed tongue-case. The moth has the fore wings slightly falcate, but not notched. They are of brown, varying from almost ocher to deep brown, and are crossed by lines of lilac and brown. Near the inner angle is a bluish-lilac patch. The hind wings are chiefly ocher-brown, with a lilac patch near the front angle, and a blue eye-spot heavily encircled with black. The head and thorax are purple-brown, with an ocher-brown stripe through the middle. The abdomen is brown, more or less suffused with lilac at the base. The wings seem to have a bloom over them when the moth is freshly emerged. The antennæ of the male are pectinate, of the female simple.

As in all the *Smerinthinæ* we know, the female is larger than the male

The eggs were all laid in July, the first lot on the 9th, the second on the 29th and 30th, and pupation took place from September 12 to October 22, the last brood being the slower in growth. No moths emerged before the following June, about the 20th.

We think *astylus* single-brooded in our part of New England, but it may be double-brooded farther south, where the warm weather comes earlier.

The ideal place for *astylus* larvæ is an old pasture or roadside where clethra, blueberry, dangleberry, inkberry, holly, "swamp-alder," and *Viburnum lantanoides* are crowded in a tangle with bayberry, beach-plum, andromeda, laurel, and azalea, with an occasional pitch-pine and soft maple rising clear of the crowd. It is an ideal place for other crawlers too — *thysbe* on viburnum, *Dolba hylæus* on inkberry, *chœrilus* on azalea, *scapha* on bayberry, *Lagoa crispata* and *Sphinx kalmiæ* on beach-plum (which is also food for *cecropia*), *Eacles imperialis* on pine and maple, and *polyphemus* on maple; while in the more open parts the sweet-fern creeps in, offering very good chance of *Sphinx gordius*. Such treasure-places we know well, and pass through them to the marsh for mignonette-scented pogonias in June, and for cranberry-vines, with berries of every color from apple-green through yellow to deep crimson, in September. From one clump of willows *excœcatus* leans toward us, while *geminatus* and *luna* may be feeding on every poplar and white birch in sight, and the folded leaves of the sassafras tell where the butterfly caterpillars, *troilus*, have been or are — "puppy-dogs" the children always call them, though to us they were more like tadpoles in shape.

"Up the Lane" leads to these tangles, pastures, and the marsh, and is our best hunting-ground — a sort of annex to the Crawlery. It never looks twice alike, and the walk back often shows us crawlers we failed to find on our way "up." We could lengthen the list of crawlers found there,— more than double it, we are quite sure,— but lists are tiresome, and enough has been said already to make any caterpillar-hunter long for that Lane.

Cressonia juglandis.

CRESSONIA JUGLANDIS

GENUS, CRESSO'NIA (named for Cresson).
SPECIES, JUGLAN'DIS ("of walnut-tree").

The eggs of this species were sent to us by a friend, and we think that *juglandis* cannot be common in Massachusetts, because we have found but one caterpillar and not one moth. It is said to be common and double-brooded near New York, however.

The eggs were ovoid and pale green. They grew yellow on the seventh day and hatched on the eighth. A second brood the following year had an egg-period of seven days.

The young caterpillars were pale yellow and rough, with short, rough, yellow caudal horns, and anal props projecting in long points behind, like those of *modesta* and *myops*. They ate butternut, and grew rather more than most sphingid larvæ in the first stage.

One brood molted on the fourth day, the other on the third, and they were about half an inch long. The head was triangular, green, with a long point on the apex, and rough with granules. The body was green, roughly granulated, with white subdorsal lines from head to horn. The legs, props, and horn were green, but the horn grew brownish in two days. There were faint yellow obliques, and the anal props were edged with whitish green. The first segment seemed to push forward over the head like a hood.

The second molt came in six days for one brood, in four for the other. The point on the head now proved to be double, became brown, and from it a brownish line extended down the back of the head, which was green, granulated with yellow-white, and had yellow face-lines. The body was green, granulated with yellow-white, and had yellow subdorsal and oblique lines. The horn was rough and brownish, the feet and props were green.

The first brood molted again in five days, the second in four. The head grew more pointed and was green, with white face-lines and brown, bifurcated apex. It was held bent so that the long points were in line with the dorsum, thrust forward like feelers. The body was green, thickly granulated with yellow-white, and had two white tubercles on the anal shield. The oblique and subdorsal lines were faintly yellow. The legs and props were green, and the horn was brown, long, slender, and depressed, so that it continued the line of the dorsum in the rear, as the head did in front. The general effect of the caterpillar was long and slender.

The fourth molt followed in seven days for one brood, in six for the other, and the change was marked, because the head was much less pointed, though still shaped like an apple-seed, with two reddish granules at apex. The anal shield had a black line from the point upward between the two white tubercles. The spiracles were red. The body now was largest at the seventh segment, tapered slightly to the anal end, and tapered much to the head, which was very small

Cressonia juglandis.

in proportion. A week later the white granules of the body were set each in a purple-brown circle, the circles being wider around the granules forming the obliques.

The caterpillars fed for twenty-one days after the last molt, then lay on the bottom of the tin for nine days, when pupation took place. They were about three inches long. Out of doors they go into the ground.

The pupa was an inch and a quarter long, rather slender, and of a black-brown. The head had four rough points, two on the apex, two just below in front. The eye-covers were studded with rough points, smaller than those on the head. The antennæ-covers were roughly serrated. The tongue-case was concealed. The last few abdominal segments had projecting rough points, which are of use in preventing the pupa from slipping back when working its way to the surface of the earth for the moth to emerge. The last segment is flattened and compressed, instead of tapering gradually, as most pupæ do.

The moths are not specially attractive. The color is fawn or ashes-of-roses, sometimes having a pinkish tinge. The wings are crossed by lines of darker brown. The males are usually darker and smaller than the females, and their fore wings are less notched. Their antennæ are widely pectinate, almost feathery.

The eggs were laid in July, the pupæ were formed in September, and the moths emerged late in the following June.

Juglandis will eat black walnut, English walnut, butternut, hickory, and ironwood, according to the entomologists. Butternut and English walnut succeeded best with ours.

They are very satisfactory caterpillars to rear, because they are, as far as our experience with three or four broods goes, very free from disease, do not entangle each other in " spin," and seldom crawl over or otherwise interfere with each other. They eat and drink as if they fully realized eating and drinking to be their business in life, and One of Us was kept busy providing fresh and succulent leaves one very dry summer. The only way of getting good ones was to pick the best she could find and put the freshly cut stems in water long enough to supply moisture to the leaf-pulp. This plan often works well in very hot, dry seasons, when without it the caterpillars would not thrive on the dry leaves.

XI

HEXAPODA

CLASS,   HEXAP'ODA   (" six-footed ").
ORDER,   LEPIDOP'TERA   ("scaly-winged ").
SUBORDER,   HETEROC'ERA   (" not clubbed antennæ ").

FAMILY ARCTIIDÆ

FAMILY,   ARCTI'IDÆ   (" furry, bear-like ").
SUBFAMILY,   ARCTII'NÆ   (" furry, bear-like ").

MOST of the arctians are rather small moths, with broad wings and thick bodies, and the caterpillars are more or less densely hairy, the " woolly bears " being the best known, perhaps. The sex of the moth can usually be told by the difference in the antennæ.

205

HALESIDOTA CARYÆ

GENUS,   HALESIDO'TA   ("chain-like": perhaps refers to the bands).
SPECIES,   CA'RYÆ   ("of hickory").

Caryæ is not a woolly bear, but is quite as densely covered with hairs and crawls quite as fast as any woolly bear. It is "the white caterpillar with a row of black buttons down its back," so often seen on elm, hickory, raspberry, willow, apple, and other trees and shrubs, on the piazza, the screen-door, the awning, and the sidewalk. It drops on one's clothes and promptly makes for one's collar and neck, traveling at racing speed, and clinging tenaciously when captured and about to be removed. It is very pretty, and very common "from Maine to the Southern States," Dr. Packard says, and really feeds on "almost everything."

We found a mat of hemispherical white eggs on the under side of a thorn-leaf, a hundred eggs set close together. They must have been laid for some time, for the next day they grew lead-colored, with red streaks, and showed the heads of the larvæ as black dots.

The next day they hatched, and the crawlers were not much like the full-grown *caryæ* caterpillars. The body was dull white, with a black patch on the dorsum of the first segment, and a black dot on each side below

the patch. The other segments had three black dots on each side of the dorsal line, set in a wide V with the point foremost, and another dot on the stigmatal line. The anal shield was black, like the head; the anal props were slender, and white dotted with black. The feet were black, the abdominal props white. All the black was highly polished. The sparse hairs were black.

The caterpillars lived in a close crowd, eating in lines on the same leaf. At this stage they ate only the green parenchyma, leaving behind skeleton leaves showing where they had fed. They drank water thirstily.

In four days they spun a web on a leaf, fixed their anal props firmly in the silk, and on the next day molted for the first time. They were very little longer than before, not measuring a full quarter of an inch. Their heads were very shining black, their bodies white with black dots, and their hairs were sparse, black and white. The first segment had the black dorsal patch, and the second and third had each two large black warts on each side of the dorsal line, and one wart on the stigmatal line. The anal segment had two large warts, also black. The hairs were longest near the head. The white of the body was like porcelain.

The little caterpillars were very active, and crawled so fast whenever the box was opened that it took both of us to clean the box, put in fresh leaves, and keep the caterpillars from escaping over the edge. Yet when the fresh leaves were in and the box closed, they all collected on one leaf as before, and fed in rows.

In five days they spun a second web over a leaf and fastened their anal props in it, and two days later they molted, leaving rows of empty skins like little sheds. This time they were over a quarter of an inch long. Their heads were round, shining black, slightly bilobed. Their bodies were as before, except that the hairs were denser and longer, being longest over the head and anal end. They now lived in two close groups, one on each side of the leaf, and still ate only the green part. They moved very rapidly and crawled under the leaf when the box was opened.

Four days later they spun a third web for molting, and in two days molted. Their heads and bodies were as before, except that on the fourth segment the black dot nearest the dorsal line on each side gave rise to a long "pencil" of black hairs, that is, hairs grouped as in a paint-brush, often called a "camel's-hair pencil." These two pencils united over the dorsal line, forming one, and on the dorsum of each segment behind the fourth were two short black pencils, united in one in the same way. These made the "black buttons down the back." On the fourth segment was a long single pencil near the stigmatal line on each side. All the other hairs were now clear white, longer than before, and longest over the two ends.

The caterpillars now ate through the leaf, and only the largest veins and midrib were left. They no longer kept in close groups, but were still gregarious. We divided them in four boxes, and had hard work to keep all in when a box was opened.

In five days they molted for the fourth time, with very slight web-spinning beforehand. The only change was that they were more densely hairy. Seven days later they molted for the fifth time, and were nearly an inch long, unchanged in marks.

In eight days the sixth molt occurred. The caterpillars were now one and one eighth inches long, had black, shining heads and legs, dull black venter and props, and the hairs were as dense as the pile of the best plush or velvet. The first segment had four black pencils, the second and third had each four long white pencils, the tenth had two long black pencils on the stigmatal lines, and the eleventh and twelfth had each two long white pencils. On the dorsum, pressing against the black dorsal pencils on each side, was a dense, short white pencil. There was a transverse black line between every two segments.

They ate voraciously for nine days, and were an inch and a half long when they began to spin their cocoons.

The cocoons were an inch long, egg-shaped, not very stiff, but opaque, and were ornamented by the hairs of the black and white pencils, shed at this time, so that the finished cocoon was like a gray egg, very symmetrical and pretty. Close examination of the cocoons showed that the short hairs had been pushed through the silk and protruded at right angles to the cocoon, giving an even surface like that of a closely cut lawn or a bit of velvet.

The pupæ formed in four days and were of a bright yellow-tan color, five eighths of an inch long, and stout, the abdomen larger in girth than the thorax.

We were not sorry when these pretty caterpillars were safe in their pretty cocoons, for in their latter

14

stages they had given us hard work to keep them where they belonged, and some of the children used to beg to " come in and see the white circus " when we opened their boxes, for we seldom escaped without at least one crawler up a sleeve or on our aprons, until we established a transfer-box, into which we put old leaves and *caryæ*, shutting them up tight, while we prepared the box and fresh twigs. Even then the changing back was not without excitement, for we did not care to put all the old leaves back, and sorting these out gave time for races between *caryæ* and our fingers, and sometimes the visiting children were called into service.

We put away the cocoons on September 20, with a relieved " *That 's* over," and on going to the cocoon-box on the 28th were amazed to find every moth out. They ought to have stayed quiet until the next June, according to the books, but there they were, having lived from egg to moth in about twelve weeks.

What could we do with one hundred *caryæ* moths ? If each pair laid at least a hundred eggs their caterpillars would ravage the neighborhood, and we knew that our one mat of eggs held a hundred, and that the moth doubtless laid a mat in a different place on each of four or five nights, which would make a goodly number of eggs even if the later mats were smaller. Moreover, we could not be sure that she laid only one mat each night. We began by killing two males and two females as specimens, and then decided that it was so late in the season that the caterpillars could not grow up before frost killed off their food-leaves, so we let the moths fly. There has been no marked increase of *caryæ* in the place, so we think that our reasoning was correct.

Out of doors the caterpillars crawl down from the trees, or drop down, and spin their cocoons in the chinks of a wall or fence, under the ledge of a piazza, or in some such dry, safe place. Occasionally we have found them in crevices of the bark on a tree-trunk.

The moths are yellow-brown, with the fore wings spotted with white. The wings are thin and not densely covered with scales, so they have not the feathery look of some moths. The color varies from light ocher-brown to dark brown. They fly by night.

FAMILY LIPARIDÆ

FAMILY, LIPAR'IDÆ ("thick-bodied").

LAGOA CRISPATA

GENUS, LAGO'A ("a hare": probably refers to the furry larvæ).
SPECIES, CRISPA'TA ("crinkled," "wavy").

In August and September the bayberry and beach-plum bushes are alive with white or tawny caterpillars shaped like half a hen's egg, cut lengthwise, and laid flat side down, with a ridge or crest running lengthwise of the back. They are not pleasant to touch, for the hairs sting like nettles, though the effect does not last long. They look like small downy feathers resting on the leaves. These caterpillars are not confined to bayberry and beach-plum, but eat also blackberry, oak, apple, pear, plum, cherry, birch, sycamore, linden, sassafras, alder, willow, and hazel, and we have found them on *Andromeda ligustrina* and blueberry. We reared them on beach-plum and bayberry, however.

The eggs we found on the first day of August, bright yellow eggs, standing on one end in close rows, and so covered with scales from the moth that they looked like cream-colored corduroy. We have found them

Lagoa crispata.

on both sides of the leaves, though more on the under side.

They hatched four days after we found them, and the caterpillars looked just like the eggs, with a few white hairs longer than the body. They did not eat their shells, but began on the leaves at once. They had seven pairs of abdominal props.

In six days they molted and came out, with whiter hairs and a little longer bodies. Their unusual point is the number of props, fourteen instead of ten. They have the six thoracic legs as well.

Five days later they molted again, were about a quarter of an inch long, yellow, with transverse rows of tubercles from which sprang whitish hairs. The head hardly showed. They moved rather slowly with a wavy motion, and seemed sluggish.

After five days they molted a third time, coming out longer, broader, and whiter, and the divisions of the segments showed clearly.

The fourth molt followed in three days, and this time they were fluffy, white, almost like fine jewelers' cotton. They ate more and moved about more.

They fed for sixteen days and then molted for the fifth time, coming out tawny, or fox-colored, with the hairs rising in a ridge or crest on the dorsal line. The hairs along the sides and on the first two segments were smoky black. They were densely hairy, and their heads showed only when eating.

They fed for twelve days, grew to a length of about three quarters of an inch, a few to an inch, and then spun very tough dark brown cocoons among leaves on the tin, though the leaves were not fastened around

them, but had a net spun across, with the cocoon between net and leaf.

In these cocoons the caterpillars hibernated, as is
their habit, pupating the following spring. The pupæ
were small and stout.

The moths are very pretty, of a rich cream-color or
pale straw-color, and have the scales of the wings so set
that there are wavy lines across them, giving them a
crinkled look. They are very "woolly" or "furry"
moths, and are about an inch and a half from tip to
tip. It is the wavy look which gives their specific
name.

The hairs of *crispata* larvæ have the power of stinging like nettles, and the caterpillars should be very
carefully handled. The effect of the sting is slight
and lasts but a short time, however.

Limacodes scapha.

FAMILY LIMACODIDÆ

FAMILY, LIMACO'DIDÆ (slug-caterpillars).

LIMACODES SCAPHA

GENUS,   LIMACO'DES (slug-caterpillars).
SPECIES, SCAPH'A   ("a boat"; boat-shaped).

The first time we found these queer caterpillars, which always suggest beechnuts although they are four-sided, they were all over the bayberry and beach-plum bushes, and of all sizes. We kept many of them through the rest of their lives, and got the pretty little moths the next year, but did not try for eggs. A few years later an entomologist wrote to us asking for eggs of *scapha*, and One of Us went hunting. Nothing could she find which at all resembled any eggs we had ever had, but her attention was attracted by some almost flat scales on the under side of bayberry-leaves, and she brought home all she found. The scales were slightly raised in the middle and were very prismatic in some lights, while in others they could be seen with great difficulty, if at all. She kept two or three of them and sent the others to the entomologist, on the chance of their being what he wanted.

In due time they let loose larvæ so small that a magnifier was needed to determine their kind. They were *scapha*, though not like the full-fed *scapha* larvæ. The head was dark and drawn under the body. The body was shaped like a flat-bottomed boat upside

215

down, and was yellowish, with a row of red-brown tubercles on each dorsal edge. They did not eat their egg-shells, which were just as prismatic as before, and could not be distinguished from shells containing larvæ. The little caterpillars were given two bayberry-leaves only, because they were so small that we feared losing them if they had more surface to wander over. They could be found without using a lens, but untrained eyes never saw anything but leaves in the box until we pointed out the little crawlers, usually greeted with: "That speck! Why, I can hardly see it!" To describe them a lens was needed.

They hatched late in July, and molted nine days later. Their backs looked pitted, and the red-brown tubercles became slightly raised dots. A transverse red line crossed the middle of the dorsum. Otherwise they were not changed, and they had grown very little. They ate their skins entirely.

In eight days they molted again. The head was brown. The body was palest green, with a red-brown bar across the first segment, red-brown subdorsals from this bar to the anal end, two red-brown patches about half-way down the subdorsal lines, and two similar patches near the anal end. There were no tubercles. The head was drawn under the edge of the first segment, which had a margin of brown and was like a hood. There were no legs or props to be seen, and the pale yellowish venter was contracted and expanded, when the caterpillar crawled, with a wave-motion.

Six days later they molted a third time, the only change being in size, and that a very slight one.

Through this stage they ate only the green pulp of the leaf, either on the under or the upper side, seeming to have no preference.

The fourth molt took place five days after the third. The head was brown, very small and retracted. The body was green, very four-sided, the venter and dorsum being wider than the sides. The dorsum was flat, rising in an arch in the middle, the head and anal ends being the lowest points of the arch. It was green, yellower in the middle, the ridges brown, darker at the anal end. Two brown patches touched the subdorsal brown ridges near the middle, and four smaller ones near the anal end. The sides were blue-green, the venter was almost white. The spiracles were round and inconspicuous. The caterpillars ate through the fiber of the leaves now, and began at the edge instead of anywhere in the middle. They were still small and very inactive, remaining on one leaf until it was eaten, even when fresh leaves were put close by them.

In six days they molted for the fifth time. They came out very deep green, except the pallid venter, with a yellow dorsal line, and red or red-brown marks on the dorsum, varying with each larva. No two had just the same amount of red or marks of just the same shape. Some had two white spots near the anal end of the subdorsal ridges, others had none. One or two were wholly green. Some had considerable yellow, others none. The anal end was pointed, and a few specimens had the middle of the dorsal ridges — the apex of the dorsal arch — almost pointed, certainly angled. They varied very much in size, color, and shape, for some were much less sharply defined than others. They were not voracious eaters, and usually finished one leaf before touching another.

To find out their range of food-plants we supplied apple, beach-plum, azalea, pear, wild-cherry, oak, willow, maple, elm, and poplar, and they ate every kind, though they did not like poplar as well as any other. Bayberry they preferred, leaving every other leaf for that.

They fed for sixteen days after this last molt, growing more in this period than in any other, then turned brown or yellowish and stopped eating. The next day they began spinning their little cocoons, having been fifty-three days in passing from egg to cocoon.

The cocoons were half an inch long, tough, firm, ovoid, very dark brown, generally smooth, but having loose ends of silk which drew leaves together over the cocoon and made it look ragged when the leaves were pulled off.

The moth is light brown, having on the fore wings a spot — shaped like half the ace of spades — of deep tan-brown, with a silver line around its rear edge, which is the curved edge. The moths have no great beauty, but their range is wide, and they lay their eggs on so many kinds of trees that the caterpillars are found very often. The moths fly by night, mating, we are told by an entomologist who has bred many, about nine o'clock.

FAMILY NOTODONTIDÆ

FAMILY, NOTODON'TIDÆ ("prominents" or tooth-backed larvæ).

APATELODES TORREFACTA

GENUS, APATELO'DES ("deceptive resemblance to Apatela").
SPECIES. TORREFAC'TA ("scorched": perhaps the brown coloring of the moths).

Virtue was rewarded. We had been weeding a little in the old garden "over at the farm-house," and the sister of One of Us, who was on her knees by an obstinate weed, called: "Do you want this moth? It's a beauty, and I've never seen one like it."

We rushed to inspect it, and on the root of a rough old pear-tree was a beautiful moth which at the first glance we took for a new smerinthid, though it was smaller than any we had seen. The fore wings were ash-gray, with deep brown near the outer margin and a dark brown, velvety patch near the body, dark brown, wavy cross-lines, and a white spot near the notched apex. The hind wings were very red-brown, with a little shade of gray near the base, two dark cross-lines, and two white and dark brown bars near the inner ends of these lines. The head, thorax, and abdomen were ash-gray, the thorax having a rich, deep brown, velvety patch, and the abdomen ending in a tuft with a deep brown tip. The antennæ were very slender,

219

so we hoped for an egg-layer, and put the moth carefully into a box. We learned later that the antennæ of the male are very feathery and his coloring is deeper, and our closer look at the moth showed that it was not a smerinthid, though we had a hunt to find out what it was.

This moth was so freshly emerged that we tied her out of the window as soon as the birds had gone to roost, and took her in before daylight. To our great satisfaction, the bit of worsted with which she was tied was dotted with little pale green disks, flat and translucent, like gelatin lozenges colored with lime-juice. Cutting off the worsted, we put the moth in a box and left her in peace, and she laid many eggs.

On the seventh day the embryo could be seen curled in the egg, but it required a magnifier to see it. On the twelfth day the eggs were dirty yellowish and opaque, and the next day the caterpillars hatched. Their heads, legs, props, and body were pale yellow, and the body was densely covered with long white hairs and a few dark ones. The hairs were very long on the thoracic segments, long on the anal segment, and shorter on the others. When looked down upon, the outline of the back was, owing to the hairs, that of a hand-glass.

They rested on both sides of the sassafras-leaves, and moved as rapidly as *caryæ*. When disturbed they dropped by a silk thread ; when touched they curled up like the woolly bears. Their longest hairs were longer than their bodies. They drank eagerly and ate holes through the leaves irregularly. Their bodies grew green after feeding. Part ate ash, part beach-

Apatelodes torrefacta.

plum, and part oak, while the first boxful had sassafras.

In seven days they molted, coming out whiter and
fluffier than before, with a dorsal line of black dashes,
and a dark pencil on the eleventh segment. Some
had grayish hairs projecting over the head.

The second molt came three days later, and the
bodies were quite green, the feet and props being conspicuously white. The hair was white and dense, and
the second, third, and eleventh segments had each one
dark, long pencil on the dorsum, resembling those of
Apatela.

Five days later they molted again. They were an
inch long. One became very yellow-white, and its
pencils were tan-colored, with black tips. From each
black dorsal dash rose a short black pencil. There was
a subventral line of black dots, and a lateral line of
black arrow-head spots. The white caterpillars had
three long gray pencils as before, and gained the dorsal
short black pencils and the subventral and lateral
lines of spots. One crawler came out Maltese gray
with black pencils.

In four days they molted again, the venter being
now black and the props black with white tips. The
black marks on the body were more distinct, and instead of the arrow-head on the first two segments was
a black dash extending upward nearly to the dorsal
line. In all the molts the caterpillars ate the cast skins
entirely, except the masks. The yellow one came out
with the body black, the hairs Maltese gray, lighter
over the head, the pencils darker gray with almost
black tips, and the legs and props black with light

tips. The head was dark gray with whitish mouth-parts.

For twelve days they fed heartily, and grew to a length of two inches. All had long, silky hair, varying in color from white to silvery gray, then to dark Maltese gray, the pencils being very dark gray with black tips. The body seemed to be black, but only the venter could be seen, the hair was so dense. The props had red tips. The caterpillars moved very fast. Those eating sassafras grew faster and larger than those on ash, and molted earlier in every instance.

After this experience we often found *torrefacta* caterpillars on trees and shrubs, and once on a student-lamp in the parlor. Usually they were of the bright yellow color, a real canary-yellow, with tan pencils having black tips; but some were white,—all in the last stage,—so the variety of color belongs to the last two stages of larval life. They are very beautiful caterpillars, and certainly gave us surprises in the course of their life.

Twelve days after the fourth molt they began to shed their long hairs, whole pencils coming off at once. Then the bodies showed, black or green with a few gray spots and short gray hairs. They were very restless and crawled incessantly for a day, then rested on the tin. Out of doors they go into the ground.

In three days the pupæ cast the larva-skin, coming out bright green, with three lines of gray spots on the abdomen, but growing shining mahogany-brown. They were much larger at the head, tapering to a sharp point.

The caterpillars were thirty-five days in passing from egg to pupa, and the moths emerged the following June.

Pheosia rimosa.

PHEOSIA RIMOSA

GENUS, PHEO'SIA ("brown-colored").
SPECIES, RIMOSA ("cracked," "with chinks").

We found the eggs on a poplar up the Lane. They were small and hemispherical, opaque white in color.

After four days the larvæ ate their way out, and very tiny they were. They were whitish green, with a subdorsal row of black dots, two to each segment, and a lateral row, one to each segment. The first segment had a black raised patch and was somewhat swollen. The second and third had two large dorsal black spots. The eleventh segment had a black tubercle on the dorsum. The anal end was black, as was the head, which was also very much polished. The feet and props were black also.

Five days later they molted. The head was black above and brown on the face. The legs and props were black. The body was green, slightly striated with yellow, and had a black caudal horn.

Three days later came the second molt. The head was paler than the body, which was of a greenish-purple color, with a faint dorsal line of a darker shade. The venter was green. The spiracles were black dots encircled by white.

The third molt followed in four days. The caterpillars were slate-gray all over, some being more purple-gray than others, and all looking shiny. The anal segment was redder than the rest of the body, and the shield was rough. The horn was black, and from it were black lines extending to the last pair of spiracles. The spiracles were black encircled with white. Some of the larvæ were green through all the stages, and in the last one had a yellow substigmatal ridge.

The fourth molt followed in three days, and the caterpillars were just as after the third molt, but larger. They grew to a length of two and a half inches or a little less, and tapered from the eleventh segment to the head.

The photograph does not give a fair idea of the slender, shining caterpillar, because the only one we could find when we wanted to photograph him for the book was too near pupation and had begun to shrink.

Pupation followed the fourth molt in five days. The pupa is dark and shining, and is formed in the ground out of doors.

The food-plants are willow and poplar, and the caterpillars are found in August and September.

Beginners usually mistake the caterpillars for sphingid larvæ, because of the caudal horn. In *Pheosia rimosa* this horn starts as a tubercle, which is exactly the reverse of the process in sphingid larvæ. They have the horn when they leave the egg, if they have it at all, and in some cases, as *pandorus, abbotii,* and *achemon,* lose the horn and have a tubercle in its place in the later molts.

The moth of *Pheosia rimosa* is very pretty, white, gray, and brown, the female being darker than the male.

NERICE BIDENTATA

GENUS, NERI'CE.

SPECIES, BIDENTA'TA ("two-toothed": the dorsal tubercles are so).

We were on the lookout for eggs of *Nerice bidentata* and *Seirodonta bilineata* for an entomologist who wanted many of each, so we were examining elm-leaves with special care. Thus it happened that One of Us, standing on a corner waiting for a street-car, instinctively looked up at the leaves of a young elm whose boughs hung over the sidewalk, and there, just out of reach, spied an egg so small that she was not perfectly sure it was an egg until she held it in her hand. The umbrella would not reach the bough; the fish-line was not in her pocket, since she was not out hunting that morning: but she could not miss a chance; so she sprang up and managed to hook the bough with her umbrella-handle, just in time to lose her car and give the passengers an exhibition of jumping. She got the leaf with the egg on it, however, and pulling out her lens, examined it before putting it into the little pocket tin, never omitted from the contents of her pocket; for in early days, when she sometimes went out without it, she had been forced to remove her glove and carry it home with a crawler in each finger and two small ones in the thumb.

15

The egg was small, hemispherical, flat on the under side, greenish yellow, with a white bloom over it. Under the lens it showed honeycomb reticulation. Putting it safely away, she looked for others, but found none.

The egg hatched in four days, at noon, but the young caterpillar could not be identified at this stage. It was really exciting, for we could hardly hope to carry one larva through all its stages,—at least, the chances were against it,—and if this were *bidentata* we were—or might be, if it lived—the first to publish its history.

This much-tended crawler was less than a quarter of an inch long. Its head was dark brown, lighter down the middle. Its body was green, sparsely hairy, with a shining-looking brown spot on the dorsum of the fifth segment, a similar one on the substigmatal line of the same segment, and a dorsal one on the eleventh segment. The legs and props were shining brown, the anal props being drawn out very thin and making a taper end to the body. They were carried in the air when the caterpillar crawled, the whole end of the body, from the fourth pair of abdominal props, being raised when in motion.

The caterpillar molted in three days, August 16. It was one fourth of an inch long, with a large, nearly round, bilobed head, pale olive-green, with face-lines of darker olive, very smooth. Its body was pale glassy green, darker on the dorsum. The fifth segment had on the dorsal line a large, brown, double tubercle or prominence, and a substigmatal one on each side. The eleventh segment had a brown dorsal hump, the tenth

Nerice bidentata.

segment a brown substigmatal patch. The anal props were striped with brown; the abdominal props and legs were brown. Sparse hairs were scattered over the body. The general effect was slender.

It molted again four days later. Its head was clear, glassy green, with two brown face-lines. Its body was glassy green, almost translucent, with very few setæ, and had a faint white lateral line, a broken brown substigmatal line, a brown substigmatal patch on each side of the fifth and tenth segments. The fifth segment had a double tubercle with brown tips, the eleventh a hump as before. The fourth and sixth segments had two green warts on the dorsum. The legs were brown and shining, the props pale brown banded with darker; the anal props were very slender. When at rest the body was like a two-arched bridge, curving from the first segment in a marked arch, the abdominal props forming the middle pier, while from them the body rose in a second arch which was completed by the anal props. These touched the twig or midrib when at rest, but were raised in the air when the crawler was in motion.

The caterpillar ate the leaf at the tip, first on one side of the midrib, then on the other, and rested, usually, on the midrib.

In a day or two all the marks grew clearer, and all the segments from six to ten had each a small, brown-tipped prominence on the dorsal line. From these prominences extended, on each side of the segment, a white oblique line, the open part of the V thus made being toward the anus. On the thoracic segments a white subdorsal line appeared. Seen in profile the caterpillar had the outline of one half of a small elm-leaf, the white obliques resembling veins.

It molted for the third time on the third day from the last molt. Its head was large, round, bilobed, green, smooth, with an almost black line on each side of the median suture. Its body was green, with a broken brown substigmatal line edged above with yellow, and a double yellow stigmatal line. The thoracic segments had a double white subdorsal line. The fourth had a double dorsal hump with brown tips; the fifth had a much larger hump, yellow-green with brown tips, the brown extending down the front and back like a dorsal line; the sixth to tenth segments had much smaller similar humps; the eleventh had a large single hump with a brown tip. From these humps extended white oblique patches. The legs were green, with a dark vertical line on each, the abdominal props pale brown banded with darker, the anal props slender, long, green, with a brown stripe on each. The anal plate was shining green like the head. The spiracles were green, with a brown line on each side, and from them rayed upward white lines like veins, distinct on the green sides of the caterpillar.

On the fourth day from the last molt the crawler molted for the fourth time. Its head was large, round, smooth, shining green, with white and black face-lines. The body was very slender through the thoracic segments, then became humped or toothed or serrate, closely resembling the edge of an elm-leaf in profile, and ended in a sudden curve down to the tips of the anal props.

When full grown it seemed deep blue-green, over-

laid with opaque white in oblique patches from the
dorsal line. It grew to a length of one and a quarter
inches, and was very pretty. When in position it
might well be taken for a part of a leaf, especially seen
from the under side.

Before this we had learned that it was *bidentata,* and
we rejoiced in every day which left it thriving.

Five days after the last molt the colors grew dull,
the humps began to diminish in prominence, and the
caterpillar emptied its intestine. The next day the
humps had shrunk to the level of the body-line, and
the caterpillar was moist and contracted. It spun a
few threads, fastening a leaf to the tin, and ten days
after the last molt the pupa cast the larva-skin.

The pupa was not quite three quarters of an inch
long, was neither stout nor slender, and was dark
brown, darker on the head, thorax, wing-covers, anal
point, and bands between the abdominal segments.
The eye-covers were prominent and very smooth. The
abdominal segments were distinctly ridged on the
edge and pitted. The cremaster was long, slender,
and sharp.

We were quite triumphant when the pupa was
finally found on the 8th of September, for it was such
a great chance whether or not we could rear the caterpillar and get its life-history.

Its portrait is from a water-color drawing taken by
One of Us, and lithographed for Dr. Packard's "Mon-
ograph on the Bombycine Moths."

The moth emerged the next June. It spreads about
an inch and a quarter, has the head and front of the
thorax bright brown, the rest of the thorax ash-gray.

The fore wings are ash-gray, with a white indented line edged in front with dark brown patches, which shade into the gray. The hind wings are very pale brown. The fringes are white, cut with dark. It is not a specially pretty moth, and is not common. It is said to be double-brooded.

We have found only this one egg, no caterpillar, and no moth.

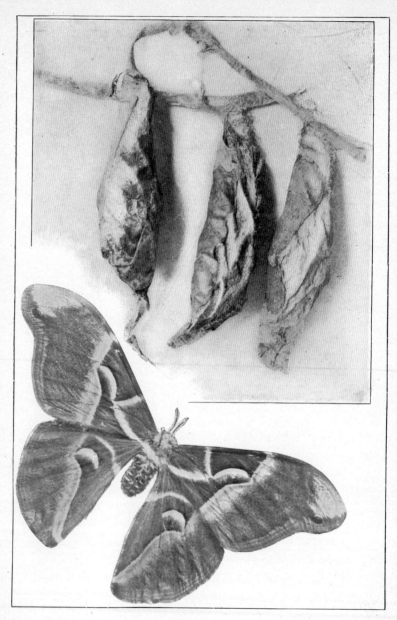

Samia cynthia.

XII

SATURNIIDÆ

FAMILY, **SATURNI'IDÆ** (children of Saturn: giants).
SUBFAMILY, **ATTACI'NÆ** (no meaning here).

SAMIA CYNTHIA

GENUS, **SA'MIA** (Samian: no appropriateness).
SPECIES, **CYN'THIA** (a name for the moon).

THERE was once a man who wished to prove that *cynthia* caterpillars spun cocoons from which could be reeled silk having as great commercial value as that of *Bombyx mori*, so he reared several thousand caterpillars and piled their cocoons in boxes in a shed, up-stairs, out of the way. In the winter he thought he would begin the reeling process, so he went for the cocoons, and found that mice had gnawed holes in all but a score or so, eating the pupæ and cutting the silken thread so many times that it was useless to attempt to reel it. About ten of the sound cocoons were sent to us, and from two moths emerging on the 8th of May we got our first *cynthia* eggs. The moth laid three hundred and forty-one eggs in nine nights, laying one hundred and fifty-nine the first night and six the last.

The eggs were chalk-white, stained more or less with the dark brown gummy fluid with which they were fixed to the netting, box, or leaf. The last eggs were pure white, the supply of fluid having been exhausted. They were ovoid, and small in proportion to the moth.

The egg-period was eighteen days, and the eggs turned lead-colored before hatching. Some were laid in even, curving lines, some in rows set in a mat, others in mats with second and third mats laid on top of the first, and a few in irregular heaps.

One set of eggs hatched in twenty-two days, one set in eighteen days, one in twelve days, and this first set we had hatched in twenty-one days.

One set of caterpillars preferred tulip-tree, one lilac, and another sassafras. They did not eat their shells.

These moths are natives of China and were imported in the hope of getting silk from the cocoons. They have become "common everywhere, especially in the cities and towns," Mr. Beutenmüller says. Their food in China is chiefly the ailantus, but in America they eat wild-cherry, linden, plum, sycamore, spicebush, sweet-gum, dogwood, holly, castor-oil plant, and a few other kinds of leaves, as well as those on which ours fed.

The young caterpillars were three sixteenths of an inch long, with polished black heads, and yellow-green bodies having twelve black dots on each segment except the first and last. The first segment had a black triangular patch on the dorsum; the last had eight black dots. On each segment were black tubercles with setæ. The legs and anal shield were black, the props yellow-green with black dots, the anal props having, each, a large black spot. They fed in rows on both sides of the leaves, all headed in the same direction.

A week later they molted, losing the black patch on the first segment, but were otherwise as before, only longer.

The second molt followed in five days. The head was now green, with two black patches, the body greener than before and five eighths of an inch long. Otherwise they were not changed.

Three days later they molted again, coming out with yellow heads, bodies of greenish yellow spotted with black, a substigmatal row of black tubercles, and two rows of yellow tubercles higher on each side. The next day the color had changed to cream-white, the yellow tubercles changing also. The legs were yellow, with black tips, the props yellow.

The fourth molt came a week later. The crawlers were larger and whiter, fed in a row on the leaf, and gave out a pleasant odor. Their bodies were covered with a waxy "bloom," which rubbed off as they moved. Their legs were yellow, with a black dot on each.

In six days they molted for the fifth time, were an inch and a half long, had greenish-yellow heads, bodies green, with black dots and a little white bloom. The tubercles were all white now, the substigmatal ones banded with black. The legs, props, and anal shield were yellow, the anal props and shield edged with light blue, and the other props with a blue spot on each. The spiracles were black, with a white dot at each end. The bodies looked slightly pitted. The tubercles grew bluish, except those nearest the head and the substigmatal row, which were distinctly blue. Some of the crawlers had all the tubercles pale blue.

In each molt they ate the cast skins.

The first ones spun nine days after the last molt, thirty-seven days from the egg. The last ones of the same brood were one hundred and five days from egg to cocoon, but were not larger than the first. The largest were almost three inches long.

They are very pretty caterpillars, and their tins are always pleasant to work over because of their fragrance. After the third molt they are very voracious, and it is no small task to provide food for a brood of three or four hundred.

The cocoon is much like that of *promethea*, which is more common, and likely to be found first by beginners. It is a deep bag with a "handle" of silk spun over the leaf-stem, and holding the stem to the twig, so that it does not fall with the other leaves, but dangles all winter unless cut off by hunters. It is usually of a weather-beaten gray, or a gray-tan color, with the upper end loosely spun, as by this the moth emerges.

We tried some experiments with our last lot of cocoons, reversing them before they were finished. If hung wrong end uppermost when the outer cocoon was still transparent, the caterpillar finished the cocoon, making the stem end the solid bottom, and leaving the cocoon loose at the end now uppermost.

Samia cynthia (after first molt and after fourth molt).

If reversed after the inner cocoon was begun, some caterpillars bit a hole in the solid bottom end, and made a loose top end of it, closing the other end. Reversed still later, some made the lower end loose, and left the upper one loose also; others merely lay with their heads to the solid end, now the upper one, and could never emerge without turning around in the cocoon.

Like *promethea, cynthia* larvæ like to draw a leaf around the sides of the cocoon, covering its upper surface, as well as the stem, with silk.

In the cocoon the pupa pushes the larva-skin down its body until it lies in a little wad at the bottom.

The pupa is stout and brown, and the antennæ-covers are so clearly marked that the male and female can be distinguished at a glance, the male having the broader antennæ. The antennæ are shaped like feathers in all these attacine moths, and are very beautiful.

The moths emerged the following spring. They measure from four and a half to nearly six inches from tip to tip, and are olive-green, with fine black scales, as if peppered. The broad band across the wings is of pinkish lilac, with an edge of black and white in places. The shorter bands are white, sometimes a little lilac. The crescents are partly yellow, partly transparent. Near the point of the fore wing is an eye-spot of black in a lilac area. The abdomen has white tufts.

These moths do not feed, their maxillæ, or tongues, being either wanting or so little developed as to be useless. This is true of all the attacine moths we have reared, probably of all. They fly at night.

ATTACUS PROMETHEA

GENUS,   AT'TACUS   (locust).
SPECIES,   PROME'THEA (Prometheus was a Titan).

We have been much laughed at for "seeing so many cocoons in impossible places," too high to be reached in any way, on forbidden grounds, in park shrubbery with a "Keep off the Grass" between the bushes and us, and in places passed in trains, far from any station; but once the laugh was on our side. On a train going out of Boston, one winter day, the Other of Us saw dangling leaves on some wild-cherry trees near the track, and not very far from a station. The train had just left this station, however, so it was too late to stop; but the next day we went back, walked along the track,— not a crime in Massachusetts, or even a misdemeanor, in that day,— and found that the heavy swinging of the leaves did mean cocoons. There they hung, scores of them! They were like *cynthia* cocoons in shape and color, and we had to cut either the stems or the silk, for the silk was too tough to break. We filled the tin box we had brought, then our coat pockets, then our dress pockets, then cut stems and all, and made bunches of cocoon-hung twigs. Every little wild-cherry in sight was treasure-hung.

It was too cold to examine the cocoons there, and

Attacus promethea.

we were inexperienced then and did not test them by weight and the "thud" when shaken, so we carried them all home and then began cutting them open very carefully to see the pupæ. Great was our disappointment on finding that most of them contained dried-up larvæ, cylindrical bundles of tiny parasitic cocoons, and empty pupa-skins from which the parasites had already escaped — probably in the autumn. From all the mass of cocoons we got but twenty or thirty sound pupæ. Still these were enough for our purposes, and when the moths emerged in June we found it easy to get all the eggs we wanted, each female laying between two and four hundred.

The eggs were ovoid, pinkish white, stained with brown, and were laid in single rows. They hatched twelve days later, toward night. The caterpillars ate their way out of the end of the shells and then crawled away from them as fast as possible, in a long procession up the stem to the tip of an ash-leaf, then to the top of the tin. Their heads were black, with a whitish stripe across the front, and a very yellow band at the back. Their bodies were yellow ringed with black, and had sparse black setæ. The legs and props were horn-colored and very conspicuous. The anal end grew black. The crawlers arranged themselves in rows on ash-leaves and ate eagerly. Six days after hatching they showed six rows of black tubercles, each having setæ spreading from its top. Just behind the head was a transverse row, or crest, of five larger tubercles, and on the second and third segments was a large tubercle on each side of the dorsal line.

On the tenth day they molted, being clear yellow at first, but becoming black and yellow as before.

On the eighteenth day they molted again. Their heads were yellow, with five black marks. Their bodies were yellow, with a dorsal line of transverse black dashes. The second and third segments had four black tubercles and two yellow ones, one on each side of the dorsal line. The others had six black tubercles, except the eleventh, which had two black ones, and one yellow one on the dorsal line, and the anal segment, which had two tubercles, connected by a black crescent over each prop.

Part of the crawlers were eating sassafras and were twice as large as those on ash, so more were given sassafras.

On the twenty-seventh day the third molt came. The caterpillars' heads were bright yellow, marked with black. Their bodies were greenish, covered with a waxy bloom which made them look almost white on the back. The first segment had two black dashes, the second and third, each, two orange tubercles, ringed with black, on the dorsum. The eleventh segment had one yellow tubercle, with a black ring. All the other tubercles were much smaller than before, hardly more than dots. The anal shield was deep yellow, with a black mark. The anal props were edged with black.

On the thirty-third day they molted for the fourth time. The only changes were in the tubercles. The orange ones on the thorax became coral-red, with black rings; that on the eleventh segment was deep yellow; the black ones were replaced by blue-black dots just raised above the level of the skin.

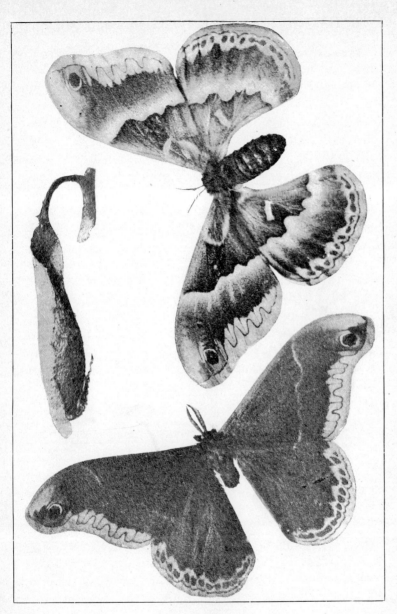

Attacus promethea.

On the forty-third day the largest caterpillars measured nearly three inches and were very plump. They began spinning their cocoons after six o'clock at night and were covered from sight the next morning.

Their cocoons were redder than those which had borne exposure to sun and rain, and when first made were nearly white.

The caterpillars were not lively after the second molt, but rested much of the time with their heads laid face down on the leaves, out of sight, as in the illustration. They are easy to rear, for they will eat apple, pear, plum, willow, cherry, lilac, ash, sassafras, tulip-tree, sweet-gum, viburnum, poplar, and various other leaves.

Promethea cocoons are considered safe from birds because they dangle so that a bird has little chance to peck holes in them, but we have found many torn open and with only the larva-skins left in them, showing that birds had eaten the pupæ. *Promethea* is very subject to parasites, but the caterpillars reared indoors from the egg are free from disease, and we have reared broods without losing one larva.

The moths are very easy to mate, for they fly at any time after two in the afternoon, and a caged female out of doors or in a window — unless the wind blows *into* the window — will draw so many males that they can be caught in the fingers as they fly or crawl about the cage. We have often drawn forty at a time, and once had all the neighbors' cats trying to catch the low-flying moths, until two dogs chased away the cats, leaving the moths to flutter in peace.

One afternoon we tied a moth out of the window, and turned away for a few moments to attend to

something else. When we went back a male *promethea*
was fluttering over an empty loop of worsted and two
female wings, and there was silence in the mountain-
ash tree where the catbird had been singing steadily
for a long time. We may wrong him. He may have
had nothing to do with it. It may have been English
sparrows. But the silence and the disappearance co-
incided.

The moths are large and vary much in coloring and
marks. The males are almost black, or quite black,
with a clay-colored border, a wavy light line across the
wings, and an eye-spot in the purplish apex of each
fore wing. They have very broad antennæ. Sometimes a male has an angular light spot on each wing,
but this is not as common.

The female has reddish wings peppered with gray,
having clay-colored borders containing reddish spots
and lines and much more noticeable cross-lines. The
apical eye-spot is very marked, and the light angular
marks are conspicuous. The antennæ are much narrower than those of the male, and the abdomen is
much larger than that of the male. Both have very
"furry" bodies and a strong odor.

Promethea is double-brooded in the South, and has
been found so in Rhode Island by one entomologist,
but all ours have been single-brooded in Massachusetts, New Hampshire, and Vermont.

Attacus angulifera.

ATTACUS ANGULIFERA

GENUS, ATTACUS (locust).
SPECIES, ANGULIF'ERA ("angle-bearing").

Attacus angulifera has been considered, by some entomologists, a variety of *A. promethea*, but experience
with several broods has convinced us that it is a separate species, and it is so considered in the Check-List.
It is a very "near relative," however, and the females
of the two species are often closely alike, though those
of *angulifera* have larger angular marks. The male
angulifera is much like the female, but is of a gray-
brown, while the female is of a red color with a yellow
tinge. They vary much in tint, some being much
redder, some very pale, others dark. The males are
usually smaller than the females, and usually are
darker. Both have the wavy light line across the
wings, like *promethea*, and the apical eye-spot characteristic of the genus. The abdomen of the male is
much smaller and his antennæ are much broader than
those of the female.

The moths mate readily in captivity and will mate
as readily with *promethea*.

Our first moths came from cocoons sent by a friend.
They emerged in July, and the eggs were laid on the
8th of July.

The eggs were like those of *promethea* in size and shape, but were pure white, and one end showed the micropyle, like honeycomb or hammered silver. This is very different from the plain egg of *promethea*, which in color and stains resembles that of *cecropia* more than *angulifera*.

On the twelfth day the eggs hatched, having become lead-colored the day before, though a few grew yellow and two green instead of lead-colored.

The little caterpillars were less than a quarter of an inch long, with dark heads banded with light stripes across the front. Their bodies were bright yellow, with a black transverse band on the dorsum of the second segment, two dark transverse lines on the anal segment, a faint dark line between every two segments; six tubercles, with setæ, on every segment except the first and last, which had four each, and the eleventh, which had five. The legs were gray-yellow, with dark tips, and the props yellow. These little caterpillars left the egg-shells uneaten and crawled to a distance before feeding.

Seven days after hatching they molted. Their heads were yellow, with a dark line and patch across the front. Their bodies were greenish yellow, with two black transverse lines on each segment; on the first segment four black tubercles with setæ; on the eleventh five tubercles, the middle° one on the dorsal line; on the other segments six yellow tubercles with yellow setæ having black tips. The anal shield had a transverse line and patch of black, and the anal segment four yellow tubercles. The legs and props were pale yellow.

Attacus angulifera (not quite full grown).

In four days they molted again. Their heads were pale green, with dark mouth-parts. Their bodies were whitish green, with two distinct black lines on each segment, the first segment having a heavy black line just behind the row of tubercles. The tubercles were as before. The feet and props were whitish green. From the head to the tip of the anal shield was a heavy substigmatal line, like a cord, of whiter green. After this molt they chose older leaves, leaving the tender ones untouched.

The third molt followed in four days. The heads were green, with a black line across the front. The bodies were very white-green, smooth, tapering from the third segment to the tip of the anal shield. The first segment had two small yellow tubercles over the head, two black dots on each side, and one over each foot. The second and third segments had two large tubercles on the dorsum, black at base, then yellow, then orange at tip; two black dots on each side and one over each foot. The eleventh segment had one large, clear yellow tubercle, ringed with black, on the dorsal line, and two black dots on each side. The anal segment had four black dots, and two black tubercles on the shield. The other segments had six black dots each. The anal shield and props were edged with yellow, and the props had each a black horseshoe mark. The legs and props were whitish green.

Six days later they molted for the fourth time. The thoracic tubercles became coral-red, ringed with black, that on the eleventh segment being yellow as before. Each abdominal prop had a black dot, and the " horseshoes " on the anal props became hollow triangles.

The yellow-white substigmatal ridge was very prominent abdominally, but gone from the thoracic segments. The blue-black dots were less noticeable than
before, and the caterpillars were very plump, smooth,
creamy-white on the dorsum, with a bloom over them,
and slightly greener ventrally.

The caterpillars were much longer when in motion
than at rest, and were rather inactive, though eating
well. They fed on tulip-tree and sassafras, and are
said to eat wild-cherry, but we never could make any
of ours touch cherry of any kind — a marked difference from *promethea*, which will eat almost anything.

Angulifera larvæ are of a creamier white than *promethea*, have much smaller dots, a smoother look, and
a very different substigmatal *edge* — for it is a corded
edge rather than a line. They slope much more from
the middle of the dorsum to the tip of the anal shield.

They fed for eleven days, growing nearly three
inches long and stout in proportion. The caterpillar
photographed was not full grown.

On the eleventh day they began spinning, and
showed another marked difference from *promethea*.
We provided twigs with leaves depending from them,
as we had done for *promethea*, but *angulifera* did not
spin any "stem" or fasten the leaf-stem to the twig.
They pulled leaves together around their cocoons, or
fastened a leaf to the tin, spinning the cocoon between the two, but in no case did a cocoon dangle
from a twig. In all we have reared, and in spite of
the different conditions provided, not one *angulifera*
has ever spun, for us, a cocoon with a stem; nor have
we ever seen such a cocoon spun by *angulifera*,

although one collector has stated that he finds such cocoons.

Out of doors *angulifera* cocoons are found among the dry leaves under tulip-trees, having fallen with the leaves spun about them. The cocoon is ovoid, about an inch and a half long, dark tan-colored, growing grayer with exposure to the weather.

The pupa is similar to that of *promethea*, and its sex may be told by the antennæ-covers, those of the male being the broader.

The moths emerged the following spring, between one and three in the afternoon.

Angulifera is more common in the Middle States than in New England, but is nowhere as common as *promethea*.

ATTACUS GLOVERI

GENUS, AT'TACUS.
SPECIES, GLO'VERI (Glover's).

This is a Western species, and we had the gray cocoons sent us in the winter. They were oval, not as large as those of *cecropia*, and with a queer, streaked look. Some were spun between leaves, others not. The outer cocoon was not much larger than the inner one, and did not separate from it easily. Both were tough, and the inner one was puckered at the top like the other attacine cocoons. From these cocoons the moths emerged early in June, mated, and the females laid many eggs, singly, in rows of four or more, and in irregular masses of ten or eighteen, just as it happened. The gummy substance which held these eggs to the leaf, box, or each other was so very adhesive that it was difficult to detach the eggs. The egg-period was eleven days, and the eggs were like those of *cecropia* in size, shape, and color.

The caterpillars began to appear early in the evening. Their heads were shining black, round, and had setæ. The bodies were black, with shining black tubercles tipped with horn-colored setæ, and noticeably long and slender. The legs and props were of the same polished black. The crawlers rested like

Attacus gloveri.

cecropia larvæ, but were longer and more slender. They ate wild-cherry, refusing the common black cherry and preferring the choke-cherry and the youngest leaves of sapling shoots. They refused to eat even the tip leaves of older trees.

In seven days they molted for the first time. The head, legs, and props were shining black. The body was dull black, with shining black, spiny tubercles. The dorsal tubercles were ringed with yellow around their base. The horn-colored setæ gave place to long, stout, polished black spines. The first segment had a pale yellow spot. A few of the caterpillars were orange, with black dots and tubercles.

They would eat common wild-cherry, *P. serotina*, but much preferred choke-cherry, *P. virginiana*, a marked contrast to *cecropia* and *promethea* caterpillars.

The second molt followed in five days. The head was small, greenish yellow with black marks, smooth, and round. The body was greenish yellow, in some cases with black dots on the dorsal line. The tubercles on the second, third, fourth, and eleventh segments were orange and black, in some cases almost black, in others orange with black spines. The other tubercles were shining black, as were the legs and props. The venter was smoky black.

They fed for but two days before molting again, and grew little. The head was green with black marks, the body blue-green on the dorsum and very yellow-green below the subdorsal lines, marked with black on the venter. There was a black line on the rear of the first segment. The tubercles on the first segment were all black, or pale blue with a black ring and top. The dorsal tubercles of all the other segments were of deep orange, changing in most cases to bright coral-red. The other tubercles were pale blue, with more or less black in most instances. Some had all the tubercles black except the dorsal ones, others had all blue, others all blue with black rings, the dorsal ones being always orange or red. The legs were yellow-green with black tips, the props either plain yellow-green or having black marks. The anal shield was very yellow-green. The spiracles were white, encircled by a very slight, dark line. The shades of green varied much, and the amount and position of black marking varied more, and in one or two cases there was no black on the body, and but slight marking on the head and feet.

Six days later they molted for the fourth time, coming out with yellow-green heads, round and large. The body was of a peculiar dark gray-green, lighter on the dorsum and very dark on the venter, except the first segment, which was light yellow-green like the head. The dorsal tubercles were all yellow with shining black spines, the others pale blue encircled with black. The legs were green with black tips, the props very yellow-green, the spiracles white. They ate part of their skins. In this stage they gave out a strong odor like camphor, and still refused all leaves but those growing on the tips of sapling shoots. This was very noticeable, for most caterpillars prefer older and tougher leaves after the second molt.

In this stage occurred the greatest loss of specimens, a loss we could account for in no way. The larvæ grew to be four inches long, and looked perfectly healthy,

Attacus gloveri.

ate well, excreted well, and suddenly were found dead. After the first death of this kind we separated them, having but one or two in each large tin; but all our care was of little use, and very few survived and spun.

They fed for sixteen days before spinning, then spun very slowly, and the cocoon was not like those which gave the parent moths, being dark brown like *cecropia* cocoons, and of a rounder, fuller shape. This was probably due to the difference of food-plant.

The life from egg to cocoon was thirty-six days.

The caterpillars closely resemble *cecropia* larvæ, and the moths have a general resemblance to *cecropia*, though smaller and far more beautiful in coloring. The head, thorax, and legs are of a deep, rosy wine-color, the collar being white. The abdomen is white with black marks in some specimens, white, black, and wine-colored in others, the amount of each color varying very much. The upper side of the wings is suffused with rich, rosy wine-color, the shade varying in different specimens, and has a white line across both wings; the borders are of clay-color, and each wing has a white crescent with a surrounding line of tan-color, then a line of black. The under side of the hind wings is of a silvery gray, and that of the fore wings is of deep wine-color.

The males are polygamous and mated with *A. angulifera* and *A. promethea* as well as with their own species. They are very active and excitable, more so than any other attacine moths we know, and the females protruded their ovipositors before their wings were half spread. They are slow in developing after emerging. Some moistened the end of the cocoon before emerging, others merely pushed through the open end. Some emerged at about ten in the morning, others in the afternoon, and one or two in the evening.

The antennæ may be black or tawny, or may have the shaft tawny and the pinnæ, or "teeth," black. The males have the wider antennæ always.

Attacus cecropia

ATTACUS CECROPIA

GENUS,   AT'TACUS   (locust).
SPECIES, CECRO'PIA (Athenian).

The big brown cocoon of *cecropia* is perhaps the most common and usually the first found by beginners, partly because it is so large, partly because there are so many, partly because they are found on so many trees or plants in such different conditions. They may be down near the root of a woodbine or syringa, under a fence-bar, on the very end of a maple-twig, along a stout branch of willow, maple, box-elder, wild-cherry, oak, apple, plum, pear, rose, currant, hop-hornbeam, beach-plum, or on the stems of swamp loosestrife growing in shallow water, making us wonder how the caterpillars ever reached these stems. We have found one flat against the stone foundation of a house. It is no wonder, then, that most of us knew the cocoon before any other stage of *cecropia*. It is a very good stage to find, for there is no difficulty in mating the moths which come from the cocoons if they emerge at the same time, or in tying out a female if no male emerges. Then one has the life-history before him, with ordinary care and good fortune.

We did not get our first history in this way, however. Ours came to us in the shape of a row of four eggs on a sweet-pea leaf. We have never been able to make a *cecropia* caterpillar eat sweet-pea leaves. Those from the eggs laid on such a leaf would not touch it, but crawled away as if it were disagreeable to them.

The eggs were ovoid, pinkish white, with a red-brown splash on the upper side, from the gummy fluid which fastened them to the leaf. They were like large *promethea* eggs, but a lens showed them pitted in wavy lines, though not deeply so.

A brood reared several years later had an egg-period of fifteen days, and the egg-layer laid three hundred and fifty-one eggs in six nights.

All the *cecropia* eggs we have found have been laid on the upper side of the leaf in short rows. In the house they are sometimes in mats and piles. The eggs grew lead-colored before hatching.

The caterpillars were fully a quarter of an inch long, all black except the props and tubercles, which were horn-colored at first. They became black later, however. On each segment were six yellow tubercles, each having seven setæ from the top, except on the eleventh segment, which had five, one on the dorsal line. The young larvæ crawled away from the empty egg-shells without eating them, and did not eat anything for twenty-four hours.

On the fourth day they molted, coming out twice as long as when hatched, but not changed otherwise.

On the ninth day they molted again, and had the dorsum dull yellow, while on the second, third, and fourth segments the tubercles on each side of the dorsal line were much larger than the others, as

Attacus cecropia.

was the one on the dorsal line of the eleventh segment.

On the seventeenth day they molted for the third time. Their heads were green, marked with black. Their bodies were yellow, with longitudinal lines of black dots; four large black tubercles on the first segment, two red ones each on the dorsum of the second, third, and fourth segments, and one large yellow tubercle ringed with black on the eleventh segment. The other tubercles were black.

On the twenty-third day they molted for the fourth time, and came out blue-green, with the red and yellow large tubercles as before; but the dorsal black ones had become yellow, and the lateral and stigmatal black ones pale blue, all with short black setæ.

They fed for ten days, growing very large around and fully four inches long, and eating voraciously. Then they emptied their intestines of a very viscous fluid and began spinning cocoons each one lengthwise of a twig, fastening the leaves around the cocoon irregularly, not drawing one leaf smoothly as *promethea* does. The cocoons were white and shining at first, then grew just the color of auburn hair. Out of doors this color grows grayer with exposure to sun and rain. They are double, the outer being loosely spun, the inner very firm and tough, almost hard.

The cocoons vary much in shape, as the illustration shows, and this variation has given rise to theories. One man considers that all the baggy cocoons contain female moths, which we have often found not to be the case. Another man thinks that the baggy ones are always found low down near the ground. We, and several other persons, have found them high on the trees. Examination of over three hundred cocoons proved to us that as many males as females, in proportion, came from baggy cocoons, and as many females as males from slender cocoons, and that both baggy and slender ones were found low down and high up. Another writer calls the baggy cocoons "the lowland form" and the slender ones "the hillside form," but we have found both forms on one tree, and even on one twig.

The only way in which we have ever been able to tell male and female pupæ, without opening the cocoons, has been by weight. As far as we have tested them in this way, the heavier cocoons held female pupæ and the lighter ones male pupæ, but we have not yet reached a point of certainty which would let us dare to say that this was a sure test. We have always found the males less numerous than the females.

The cocoons found vary in color, even before they have "weathered," and we once had a *cecropia* larva spin a cocoon which was silvery white at first, then of an exquisite pale green. It has faded somewhat in the course of years, but is still green, the only one we have ever seen or heard of, though the silkworms often spin green cocoons in Italy.

The egg-period varies, being sometimes three weeks. The length of larval life also varies from four weeks to eight or nine.

Box-elder is a favorite food-plant, but we have had best success with apple, wild-cherry, and willow, and the largest *cecropia* we ever saw was found on a willow in a swamp.

Attacus cecropia.

Country people often tell us how badly *cecropia* caterpillars bite or sting. This is utterly impossible from their structure, and we have handled hundreds of them with no such experience.

The pupæ have very marked antennæ-covers, and their sex is easily told by them.

The moth is our largest spinner. Its head and thorax are red, a rusty red; the collar is very white; the abdomen is red, with bands of white and black. The wings are pepper-and-salt or iron-gray, with a cross-band of black, white, and red; the apical eye-spot is in its purplish patch on the fore wings, and there is a crescent of white, bordered with red and black, on each wing. The wings are bordered with clay-brown, much grayer on the under side. The antennæ are broadly pectinate.

These are superb moths, with very furry bodies and legs. They fly late, never mating, as far as we can learn, before twelve o'clock, and usually not before four in the morning. They do not feed, as their maxillæ are not developed. They may be caught near electric lights or lighted windows, and will fly into open windows if a bright light is in the room. They are sometimes found under shed-roofs by day, and may be tracked to their hiding-places by their strong odor, especially strong in the females. The easiest way of getting them, however, is by collecting the cocoons in winter, or, better yet, as early as possible after the leaves fall in the autumn, before the birds go cocooning. Blue jays eat the pupæ of *cecropia*, and so do some woodpeckers, but we have never seen the caterpillar touched by any bird. Jays, robins, and

English sparrows we have seen eating the moths,
though the sparrows had a hard struggle to dispose of
the flapping wings, which seemed to bewilder them.
When the wings were bitten off, the body was quickly
eaten in spite of its furry scales.

Cecropia caterpillars fall victims to at least three
kinds of parasitic flies — *Ophion* and *Cryptus extrematus*, which are ichneumon-flies, and *Microgaster*, a
braconid genus.

Ophion deposits one egg under the skin of the caterpillar, and the grub from this egg feeds on the
caterpillar's tissues until the larva is ready to pupate,
having spun its cocoon. Usually a cocoon spun by a
stung caterpillar is thinner and lighter in color than a
normal one, but this is not always the case. Comstock
says that larvæ stung by *Ophion* do not pupate, but the
Ophion larva does, making a large, oblong, round-
ended cocoon, very tough and of a rich brown color.
We have often found them in the cocoons of *cecropia*
and *polyphemus*. The fly has an orange body and
iridescent wings.

Cryptus extrematus is smaller, and lays many eggs in
one caterpillar, piercing the skin with her ovipositor.
The grubs feed and spin cocoons inside the cocoon of
their dying or dead host.

The little braconid flies deposit their white eggs on
the outside of the caterpillar, and often many on one
larva. When the grubs hatch they eat through egg-
shell and caterpillar-skin into the body of the crawler,
and there feast until ready to pupate, when they eat
through the skin, stand on their anal ends, and spin
little white or yellow-brown cocoons which stand out

Attacus cecropia, ♂.

all over the body of the caterpillar. Usually the caterpillar lives until the cocoons are spun, but in the latter days of its life it is inactive and suffering, does not eat, and writhes painfully.

These braconids are found on many species of caterpillars, both sphingid and saturniid, even on the small larvæ of some noctuid moths.

Once in a while a caterpillar is found with only two or three eggs on its skin, and its life may be saved by crushing or removing the eggs with forceps or a knife, if the grubs have not left them for the body of the caterpillar.

It is not always possible to tell a stung larva, because the egg-shells are cast with the molted skin, and the eggs of the ichneumonids are under the skin. Before the braconids come out to spin, however, they may be seen moving about just under the thin skin of the caterpillar.

These are all hymenopterous flies, but there are also dipterous flies which prey upon caterpillars of many kinds, *cecropia* among the rest. These are the Tachina flies, which look like very large, hairy house-flies, and their larvæ make short, red-brown, round-ended pupæ. The eggs of these flies are laid on the skin of the caterpillar, many on one victim. We have often found the egg-like pupæ in the box of a choice and treasured crawler on whom our hopes were set.

SATURNIINÆ

SUBFAMILY, SATURNII'NÆ.

ACTIAS LUNA

GENUS,   AC'TIAS   (a Greek proper name).
SPECIES, LU'NA   (the moon).

Luna lays eggs as purely white as its own white scales. They are much like those of *angulifera* in size and shape, and ours have been laid in rows, not many in a row. We have had many eggs of *luna*, and never one which was not white, though one writer describes them differently. They grow lead-colored before hatching. Out of doors they are laid on twigs or the upper side of leaves.

The egg-period has been three weeks, but probably varies with the hot or cold season, as does that of other moths.

The caterpillars were a quarter of an inch long, tapering from head to anus. Their heads were green, marked with black across the front. Their bodies were yellow-green, the anal plate being bluer. The first segment had four large tubercles with yellow setæ. The other segments had six smaller tubercles

Actias luna.

with setæ. The legs and props were green. The empty shells were left untouched, and the caterpillars preferred oak to any other leaves provided.

On the tenth day they molted. Their heads became green, with two brown spots. The dorsal tubercles grew reddish. These were the only changes except increased size.

On the fourteenth day they molted again. This time the head was all green, with red-brown mouth-parts; the legs and props were red-brown at tip, the tubercles were yellower than the body, and a yellow substigmatal line extended from head to anus.

On the twenty-first day they molted again. The tubercles had yellow tips; the yellow substigmatal line became conspicuous; a yellow line appeared on the anal plate and props, and a transverse yellow line on the hind edge of each abdominal segment. Their bodies were of a clear yellow-green, darker below the lateral line and on the venter.

On the twenty-eighth day they molted for the fourth time, having no change of colors or marks.

On the thirty-seventh day they passed a fifth molt, and were unchanged except that their colors were brighter. Some had bright red tubercles; some had yellow tubercles on the dorsum of the second and third segments, and the rest blue with yellow tips. Some had pale brown heads. Some were very blue-green as they grew nearly full fed, others were golden green. Some broods preferred hickory, some birch, others oak, butternut, and walnut. We hear that sweet-gum is a very favorite food for *luna*, but we have not tried it with them. We have found them on willow.

The caterpillars are rather delicate as they grow older, having some disease which causes black spots near the tubercles, or some of them, and usually proves fatal. A larva thus affected should be removed at once, as one seems to infect the others.

On the fifty-fifth day the caterpillars began spinning, having first become orange-pink on the dorsum. They were three inches long. As soon as a crawler turned pink we put it by itself in a box with leaves that the others might not disturb it.

The cocoons were brown, ovoid, rather irregular, very thin, and had no loose end, as have those of *cecropia* and *promethea*, nor were they double, as those are. Leaves were spun around each cocoon. Out of doors the caterpillar crawls down the tree and away from it, and spins its cocoon among leaves on the ground.

Luna caterpillars are not found on the walks and roads as often as *polyphemus*, probably because nut-trees are less often planted by the roadside than are maples. We often find them on white birch and oak, especially on young trees.

The moths are common almost everywhere, though there is a popular belief that they are rare. Probably this is due in part to their food-plants, being forest trees, less often planted near houses, and to the late hours of the flying moths. Our naturalist doctor tells us of seeing them around lights in a piece of wooded road he has had to pass over between two and three o'clock in the morning.

The moths are of an exquisite pale green color, the costa of the fore wings being purplish, and the color

Actias luna

extending across the thorax. Near the body there are long furry scales of purest white, and the fringes of the wings may be white, yellow, or red. On each wing is a transparent spot edged with white, black, and sometimes red. The hind wings are drawn out in long "tails." There are no apical eye-spots. The antennæ are very pectinate, and those of the female are the narrower.

Luna is considered to be double-brooded, but ours laid eggs early in June, the larvæ fed until the latter half of August, then spun, and no moths emerged before the following spring, though the cocoons were kept in a room warm enough to sit and work in.

Luna moths do not eat. Their pupæ are the noisiest we have ever had, for they rustle like fallen leaves. One will start squirming in its cocoon, and that seems to start all the rest, with the result that they can be heard across a large room. One of Us has risen and gone to see if a mouse could possibly have got into their box, and this more than once, though mice are less common than *lunas* in the house.

TELEA POLYPHEMUS

GENUS,   TE′LEA   ("the end": no appropriate meaning).
SPECIES, POLYPHE′MUS (a giant).

The caterpillar is found most often, next perhaps the moths, though if one haunts electric lights the moths would probably be found most often. The cocoon is found, but not as often as that of *cecropia* or *promethea,* and we have found more eggs than cocoons.

The eggs are larger than those of *cecropia,* circular, white, with the edge brown, like two white disks bound together with a brown band. They are laid in a short row, two or three together, or singly, on the under side of a leaf or the upper side of a twig, though we have found some on the upper side of white birch leaves as well as on the under side. The brown band had a white dash across it in one place, and opposite this a white dot. The eggs grew brown before hatching, and the caterpillars ate their way out at the white dash.

Sometimes the shell did not come off the anal end, or rather the little caterpillar could not get free from the shell, and in this case the crawler seized the shell in its mouth, grasping it with its feet, and pulled and tugged until the anal props were pulled free, when the

Telea polyphemus.

shell was dropped. This happened only with shells not held in place by the maternal glue.

The caterpillars' heads were round, large, and red-brown. Their bodies were reddish over the thoracic segments, yellow elsewhere, with a lateral line of dark dots, two on each segment, and six small tubercles with dark setæ on each segment. They measured one fourth of an inch in length.

On the eighth day they molted. Their heads and legs were red-brown. Their bodies were blue-green above, yellow-green below the lateral line, with yellow tubercles. The props were green, and the anal plate was edged with white.

On the thirteenth day they molted again, coming out rather yellower than before, and looking as if the lines between the segments had been cut in deep. The tips of the tubercles and the edge of the anal plate were pearly white.

On the nineteenth day they molted for the third time, coming out as before, but over an inch long, and with the anal shield edged with brown and conspic-uous. When disturbed they made a low grating sound, which seemed to be made by rubbing the mandibles together.

On the twenty-eighth day they molted for the fourth time, and were not changed in looks. They now ate voraciously and grew to a length of fully three inches, one or two being even longer.

We have reared many broods and captured larvæ, and made many experiments with their food, and there seem to be few of our native trees whose leaves they refuse. We have found them on maple, oak, willow, elm, hickory, white birch, poplar, chestnut, walnut, beech, linden, hazel, apple, pear, wild-cherry, weigelia, pine, and wild grape, and some of our larvæ grew up on wistaria. Rose and quince are given as their food-plants, but we have not tried them. With this variety of possible food and the great number of eggs laid by each female moth, the species would over-run the land if it were not held in check by parasites, diseases, and possibly by birds. We have not seen birds touch *polyphemus*, but I am told that robins eat the caterpillars.

Ichneumonid, tachinid, and braconid flies sting the larvæ, and these are also subject to the disease of the tubercles which kills so many *luna* caterpillars. We have lost scores by this disease, and have found in the woods many so diseased.

Our caterpillars began to spin on the fiftieth day after hatching, and spun very tough, white, oblong cocoons with round ends. The cocoons were covered with a white powder like lime, and were spun among leaves. Occasionally out of doors we find a *polyphemus* cocoon spun against a twig, but not often. Usually they are spun inside a bent leaf or two and fall with them, or the caterpillar crawls down to the ground and spins among leaves.

Polyphemus is single-brooded, but the moths straggle along so that caterpillars may be found from June till late October in Massachusetts. They are very pretty caterpillars, and those with bright red, lustrous tubercles are specially clean-looking and attractive.

We were walking on a country road once, years ago, with our boxes full, and had in plain sight a twig with

Telea polyphemus.

Telea polyphemus and cocoon.

a very large *polyphemus* caterpillar on it. It was quiet and had its head flat against the twig, after the manner of the big spinners when at rest. An old farmer met us and stopped to ask: "Say, does that kind do any damage to the trees?" We said that there were not enough to do any great harm, and added: "Is n't he a beauty?" "Well, I ain't never looked for beauty in a worm before, but I swan he 's as fair an' wholesome an' noble-looking as ye are yourself."

"Noble" in that region refers only to size. Any cow, horse, pig, dog even, which was well grown and healthy was always "noble" or "noble-looking" in that part of the world, so we were not unduly "set up" by the compliment.

Polyphemus caterpillars are much like *luna*, but lack the yellow lines between the segments and on the sides, while their tubercles have a metallic luster which those of *luna* have not, and the edge of the anal shield is conspicuously brown, which is not the case with *luna*.

The cocoon is unmistakable.

The moths are large and of beautiful coloring, varying much in tint. The fore wings are of yellow or red tan-color, slightly peppered with black scales, having the costa gray. A band of white and red or pink crosses the wing near the body, and a band of gray, white, and red or pink crosses the wing near the margin. There is an apical patch of white and pink, with two black spots suggesting the eye-spots of the attacine moths. On each wing is a transparent spot crossed by a yellow line and surrounded by a line of tan-color, then one of black.

The hind wings are so much more peppered with black scales that they are darker and grayer than the fore wings. They are crossed, near the margin, by a band of gray, white, and pink or red, wider than that on the fore wings, and each wing has a large gray eye-spot, edged above with black, white, and pink or red, and inclosing on the lower edge a transparent, oval spot, crossed lengthwise by a yellow bar, and encircled by tan-color and black. The bodies are tan-colored, with a gray band across the thorax. The antennæ are very broadly pectinate, the male's being the wider. The shades of tan, red, and gray vary very much in different moths, but all are very furry. They lay many eggs, but diseases and parasites kill most of the larvæ.

A friend once sent us a tin box, about six inches long and two in diameter, by mail. It was four days on the way, and when we opened it we found a large *polyphemus* moth, apparently dead, and over three hundred eggs dotted all over the inside of the box and cover. While we were removing the eggs the moth was left on the table, but when we went to get her she had revived and flown to the window-curtain. That night she laid more eggs, and the next night we set her free to enjoy the rest of her life in her own way.

These moths are often found on the ground under electric lights, apparently displaying their beauty to all whom it may concern.

Hyperchiria io.

HYPERCHIRIA IO

GENUS,   HYPERCHIR'IA ("she who protects"; a surname of the goddess Hera:
                no meaning here).
SPECIES,   I'O   (a priestess of Hera beloved of Zeus).

Going up the Lane one day, we found on a bayberry-
bush a group of thirty eggs, or rather three groups
close together. The eggs were top-shaped and stood
on the pointed end. They were opaque white in color,
with a yellow band, and a black dot on the top of each.
Afterward we found that the new-laid eggs were white,
with a dim yellowish spot on top. In ten days the
yellow band had become brown, and the dark dots
showed themselves to be heads, the shells being now
transparent.

On August 4 the eggs hatched, giving tiny caterpillars with almost black heads and tan-colored
bodies, having six tubercles on each segment. These
tubercles were set with radiating spines, which stung
like nettles through all the larval stages. The little
crawlers left the empty shells, formed in a single line,
and marched in procession along the stem to the top-
most leaf, there settling in rows to feed. Wherever
they went, one led and the rest followed. The leader
spun a thread which seemed to serve as a guide to the
second crawler, who also spun a thread. Sometimes

the third or fourth caterpillar would feel the thread with only one palpus and so walk along at one side of it, spinning his own thread parallel to it; then the next larvæ would find two threads, and the procession would march by twos. Sometimes other caterpillars still farther back would follow at the side of, instead of on, the threads spun, and their parallel threads would widen the ranks still more, until it was a wedge-shaped mass. In any case it was a funny sight to see these small caterpillars following a leader along stems and leaves to feed, and back again to rest. We could not make out whether it was always the same leader, or how the leader started his followers. There seemed to be no communication between them, and unless the vibration of the leaf or stem, when the leader started, aroused the others, we could see no way of doing it.

For eight days they marched and fed, then molted, and were just as before, but larger.

They fed and marched, and rested in rows for two weeks more, then molted again. This time their heads were black, their bodies brown, with a sublateral band of lighter brown edged with white lines. The spines were black and dense, the legs dark, the props light brown. Toward the end of this stage they began to scatter over the leaves and stopped marching.

In seven days they molted, coming out pale green all over, except the brown and white sublateral stripes, and a few black spines among the green ones.

Eight days later they molted for the fourth time, and were pale green, with the brown and white sublateral bands, a substigmatal line of brown patches, and brown speckles on the anal props. The green spreading spines gave the caterpillars a mossy look, and urticated, or stung, well if touched. This is not by any volition of the caterpillar, but because the pressure on the spines forces out the acid secretion which causes the stinging sensation.

Io caterpillars sometimes live on corn, and many a country man and woman will tell of being bitten by "an awful green bug" on the corn when they have rubbed against an *io*.

They began spinning on the fifty-seventh day after hatching, having grown to a length of two and a half inches.

We often find them on willow, beach-plum, bayberry, wild-cherry, apple, pear, plum, hickory, sassafras, elm, maple, oak, birch, and linden, and they have been found on locust, ash, poplar, rose, currant, and clover, and "many other plants." They are common everywhere, but do not seem abundant enough to do any real damage, though we once saw a small willow defoliated by twenty-one *io* caterpillars. They are single-brooded, but the moths have often disappointed our hopes by emerging in November or December instead of waiting till spring — summer rather, as they are due in July.

The cocoon is very thin — so thin that the pupa can be seen through it — and brown. It is much like the cocoon of *luna*, but is thinner and more shapeless. It is spun among leaves on the ground. The pupa is short, stout, almost black, and has a cremaster furnished with hooks which hold it in place in the cocoon. The broad antennæ show the male as in other saturniids.

The moths are much gayer in colors than the others of their family. They are not alike. The male is bright yellow, the fore wings having a wavy line and marks of purple-brown; the hind wings being red-purple near the body, and having a large eye-spot of black with a blue pupil crossed by a white line. This eye-spot is surrounded by yellow, then a black line, then yellow, then by a band of red-purple uniting the areas of that color on the fore· and hind edges of the wing. The outer margin of the wing is yellow.

The female is tawny of body, and has the fore wings of a purple-brown of varying shades crossed by wavy lines of greenish yellow, sometimes really green. The hind wings are like those of the male, except that their outer margin is pale purple-brown.

The male's antennæ are broadly pectinate, the female's very slightly so. On the under side of the fore wing of both male and female is a black eye-spot with a white central dot, and on the under side of each hind wing is a white elongated dot. These moths fly after dark, and may be taken at lights. They do not feed.

Eacles imperialis (from living moths).

XIII

CERATOCAMPIDÆ

FAMILY, CERATOCAMPIDÆ (horned caterpillars).

EACLES IMPERIALIS

GENUS, E'ACLES (no meaning).
SPECIES, IMPERIA'LIS ("imperial").

WE had found some of these large, horned caterpillars in the autumn, and in June of the next
summer the moths emerged and mated, and eggs were
laid — about two hundred eggs by each female. The
moths fly late, and they mated after nine o'clock,
probably much later.

The large yellow eggs were laid singly on the upper
side of leaves. They were like drops of honey or clear
amber, and grew browner before hatching. The egg-
period was thirteen days.

Eggs of *Eacles imperialis* had a red line part of the
way around the edge of each. As the larva developed,
this line became broken, and, on the day before hatching, showed the red dashes to be the dorsal tubercles
of the larva. This could be seen without a lens, but a
fifteen-diameters glass showed also the setæ at the top

271

of each tubercle, those on the four tubercles over the head being black, the others white. When the larva hatched, the red raised dots—for they were not more than that—began to grow at once, the red color remaining in the tip of each, and the lower part having almost no color at first. The growth was so rapid that in five minutes after leaving the shells the long thoracic tubercles or "horns" had their normal size and shape, and the lateral spines had appeared. The setæ grew dark first, then the spines, then a pale red color suffused the horn, as if it ran down from the tip, which grew paler.

The abdominal tubercles gained the normal color first, in about fifteen minutes, and in an hour all the tubercles, spines, feet, tips of props, and mouth-parts had become black.

The development of the long tubercles was very rapid and very interesting, and was watched in many instances, each one giving exactly the same details in the same order, though the caterpillars differed much in the time they took to eat their way out of the shell, some needing an hour, others over two hours.

Observation of another set of eggs showed that the color of the thoracic setæ varied, some larvæ having the setæ all black before hatching, others having only those of the first segment black, the others being white.

The little caterpillars were nearly a quarter of an inch long, deep ocher-yellow in color, with black transverse lines on the dorsum, except on the thoracic segments. The first segment had two prominent tubercles and four small ones. The second and third segments

Eacles imperialis (green larva).

had each two horns on the dorsum, bifurcate and with white tips. The eleventh segment had one long horn and four tubercles with setæ. The other segments had two short dorsal horns and one on each side. The anal segment had two large tubercles or horns and several small ones. The legs and props were black. There were sparse hairs all over the body. They ate part of their shells.

On the fifth day they molted, the color growing chocolate-brown.

On the ninth day they molted again. Their heads were large, round, with two dark brown marks. The anal shield was very conspicuous, being tan-colored, with three branching tubercles. The horns on the thoracic and eleventh segments were much longer and more noticeable, light with dark tips. There was a dark dorsal line. The spiracles were very conspicuous, set in pale brown ovals.

On the fifteenth day they molted again. Their heads were brown, with darker face-lines. They had long white hairs, sparsely scattered over the dorsum and substigmatal regions, and shorter, closer ones on the sides. The anal plate and props were very horny, black dotted with white and edged with ocher-yellow, polished like hard rubber. The spiracles were oval whitish spots set in dark brown. One caterpillar came out bright green, with a pale yellow head having dark brown face-lines, and its anal plate and props were edged with pale yellow. All had the second, third, and eleventh segments much humped under the horns.

On the twenty-second day they molted for the fourth time. The green one had the head cream-colored, with black face-lines and edge-lines, and the feet cream-colored, with black at their base. The body was green, with long sparse white hairs. The spiracles were white encircled with blue-black, large, oval, and conspicuous. The anal plate and props were black, dotted with white and edged with cream-color. The abdominal props were green. The brown ones had the heads brown, with darker lines; the bodies brown, with a dark dorsal line, and the sides darker than the back. The legs and abdominal props were dark brown; the anal plate and props were shining black, dotted with white and edged with light brown. There were long white hairs. The spiracles were dark with a white line, set in ovals of light brown, not as conspicuous as those of the green one.

On the thirtieth day they molted for the fifth time. The horns and tubercles were less noticeable, as if they had shrunk or the caterpillars had "grown up to them." The green larva was dark bottle-green speckled with lighter, and had fox-colored hairs. The brown ones were as before. They ate well and grew to be over three inches long, and stopped eating on the fifty-first day.

Usually the caterpillars are more to be noticed on account of the horns on the thorax and their marked anal props and shields than on account of their hairs, but one year we found several green ones like the very hairy one pictured. These looked so unlike the common ones that they seemed almost a different species, or at least a variety. The photograph of this one is perfect. The dark photograph is of a very dark brown larva, more common than the green hairy form.

Out of doors they burrow in the earth to pupate,

Eacles imperialis (brown larva).

but they have always transformed perfectly in our tins without any earth, or on a shallow layer of sand if a box happened to have sand in it.

The pupæ are stout, black, and rough with projecting spines which help the pupa in working its way up to the surface when the moth is to emerge.

The caterpillars do best, with us, on pine, junipei, and hickory. They are found on spruce, hemlock, maple, oak, birch, cherry, sumac, alder, sycamore, elm, beech, sweet-gum, and sassafras.

The moths are bright yellow, genuine canary-color, the wings being crossed by lines of the pinkish-purple color which has lately been called " heliotrope," and dotted with the same color. Near the body this heliotrope covers a broad area, or nearly covers it. On each wing is a pale spot encircled by heliotrope. The body is yellow with heliotrope patches, very clumsy and thick. The antennæ of the male are pectinate, those of the female scarcely so. The male is smaller than the female.

There is a variety with the wings so covered with dark dots as to look dark, and a second variety is found in Texas.

The moth is common everywhere, "especially in city parks," Mr. Beutenmüller says.

Pinus rigidus is the favorite food of the caterpillars near the Crawlery. They fasten their anal props on a stem, crawl up until they can clasp a tuft of needles with their legs, then bend it down and eat off the tips as a child eats a stick of candy. The caterpillars may be found by searching the branches over the great balls of excrement, and the moths can be taken at lights. They fly late.

CITHERONIA REGALIS

GENUS, CITHERO'NIA (a Greek poet).
SPECIES, REGA'LIS ("royal" or "regal").

Unfortunately, this fine and formidable-looking caterpillar is not often met with in New England, though
it is found now and then on ash, hickory, butternut,
sycamore, sumac, and walnut, while farther west and
south it feeds also on persimmon and sweet-gum.

We had never seen any stage but the moth until a
friend sent us a box of the large amber eggs, like
those of *E. imperialis*, but larger and encircled with a
red line. Under a lens they showed facets.

After a few days the eggs showed the black heads
of the larvæ, and then the segments of their bodies,
and then grew black speckled with orange. On the
sixteenth day they hatched, and in spite of the size of
the eggs, the size of the caterpillars surprised us.
They were a little over half an inch long, and their
black round heads looked huge. Their bodies were
velvety black, and on the first segment were two long,
rough horns ending in a ball from which spread horizontally two spines or setæ. Below these horns, on
each side of the larva, was a much smaller one. On
the second and third segments each were four long
horns, the two dorsal ones being much larger than

Citheronia regalis

those below them on the sides, and very much larger than those on the first segment. On the eleventh segment was one moderately long horn on the dorsal line and one on the subdorsal line. The anal segment had two small horns on the anal plate and five above it. The other segments had two short dorsal horns, two shorter subdorsal ones, and, as had all the segments, a short substigmatal horn. These were yellow at first, but grew black, having at times a reddish, horny look. On each abdominal segment was a pair of yellow oblique lines. On the sixth and seventh segments were two oval light brown patches, one on each side of the dorsal line. The legs and props were black, the spiracles to be seen only with a lens.

These caterpillars were unusually restless. They drank eagerly and ate butternut and ash. They rested curled, so that their heads nearly touched their eleventh segments, and all the thoracic horns were bent forward almost horizontally. They began eating near the edge of the leaf and ate irregular holes across the surface, leaving the midrib. They always crawled away from their feeding-place to rest.

On the fifth day they spun webs on the leaves or tin, fastened their props to them, and molted two days later. They had grown a little larger, and were of a rich red-brown color, the thoracic segments and horns being darker. All the horns were set with sharp spines, and the long ones had no ball or knob at the tip. They were lighter in color, branching, and had dark tips. There were no dorsal yellow patches, but on each side of the dorsal line were two black dashes. The light obliques — which pointed forward, instead of backward, as do those of the Sphingidæ — were edged above with black. The legs and abdominal props were dark brown, the anal props and shield hard and shining, like hard rubber. The long horn on the eleventh segment was light, with a dark tip. All the long horns could be raised and depressed at will.

The caterpillars ate every trace of their cast skins — even of the harder covering of the horns — except the masks.

On the tenth day they molted again. Their heads were deep red-brown, round, and shining, as were the legs and anal props. The abdominal props were darker. Their bodies were as before, except black patches between the thoracic segments and a black transverse bar behind the third segment on the dorsum. The long horns were light with dark tips, and branched, being set with small spines or "thorns."

They ate the entire cast skin as before. They fed separately from the outset, crawling away from each other and the empty shells.

The third molt came on the fourteenth day, and they crawled out of their skins larger and redder than before, with their thoracic horns ringed at base with black. The props were very dark, with redder lines down the sides, and their clasping tips (*plantæ*) were very bright orange.

On the twenty-first day they molted for the fourth time. They were three inches long, and had tan-colored heads with a dark band on each side. These bands extended over the dorsum of the first segment between the horns. The first segment was tan-colored, with a horny dorsal plate, and two light patches on

Citheronia regalis.

each side. There were velvety-black bands between the thoracic segments and behind the third segment. The dorsal long horns were tan at base, then black, rough, and no longer branching, and curved backward, except those on the first segment, which projected over the head. The fourth, fifth, and eleventh segments were lighter on the dorsum. The venter was very dark brown. The "obliques" were yellow, and merged in a wavy line from the fourth to the twelfth segments. The legs were tan-colored, with black marks; the props nearly black, with red lines; the anal props and shield enormous, horny, rough, tan-colored, with black marks. The spiracles were large, oval, with a light line around them.

They ate ravenously, beginning at the stem end of a leaf and mowing down great curves from edge to midrib, never eating the whole leaf, but leaving at least the last third of its length untouched, until nearly grown, when they ate all the upper part, leaving the base.

As they grew older they changed in color, some being almost green on the dorsum, with an orange plate on the first segment, and orange anal plate and props, being brown elsewhere. The horns and spines became blue-black and iridescent. Some caterpillars were yellow-brown, some red-brown, some of a queer greenish color with blue-green transverse bands.

On August 9, the thirty-third day, they measured five and a half inches in length, and were large in proportion. They stopped eating and crawled about somewhat, not nearly as much as *P. celeus* larvæ, and pupated four days later.

Instead of clasping the twig with the anal props, *regalis* larvæ, when nearly grown, fasten one prop on the other, the twig being held between them, but not by them, as a ring is around a finger.

They were very peaceful and quiet crawlers, never interfering with each other and never injuring each other.

The pupæ measured an inch and three quarters in length and the same in girth around the thorax. They were stout, smooth, almost black, with a double black horny plate on the back at the base of the thorax, and a smaller one on the eighth abdominal segment. The back of the thorax was transversely ridged. The pupæ gave out a strong and unpleasant odor, like laudanum with a tang of valerian.

Butternut makes larger *regalis* caterpillars than ash, and those fed on it were the first to molt and pupate. The differences of color, however, were not due to either food-plant, as all varieties were found in each set of tins.

Mr. Beutenmüller gives no mention of the brown larvæ in his "Bombycine Moths Found within Fifty Miles of New York," yet they have been far the more common with us, and we have seldom had a clear green larva such as he describes, though we have reared several broods, not from the same parents. He does mention a black form, which we have never seen.

The moths are of a queer orange-brown color, with stripes of lead-color between the veins of the wings, and large bright yellow spots on the fore wings. The hind wings have a yellow patch near the fore margin, and often only three or four lead-colored stripes, some-

times more. The head, thorax, and abdomen are
orange-brown, marked with yellow. The antennæ are
bright orange-brown, broadly pectinate in the male,
almost simple in the female.

Regalis is not considered common anywhere, but
has an extended range. It is said to be double-brooded
in Georgia, but not so as far north as New Jersey or
New York.

The moth is known as the "regal walnut-tree moth,"
and the caterpillar as the "horned hickory devil."

The horns are perfectly harmless, and cannot sting
or hurt any kind of enemy, yet they doubtless frighten
any bird which may be tempted by so large a morsel,
and certainly frighten many human beings, as visitors
to the Crawlery could testify. We gained a most unmerited reputation for heroic courage while we were
rearing *regalis* — unmerited because we knew the
caterpillars to be harmless.

ANISOTA STIGMA

GENUS,   ANISO'TA   ("unequal": probably from the unequal length of the
                    horns and spines).
SPECIES,   STIG'MA   ("dotted").

The mother of this life-history came out in one of our
cages, having been found in the oak-woods as a caterpillar.   She was mated and laid us many small, round-
ovoid, orange eggs.   This was early in July.

The eggs grew brownish, and the heads of the larvæ
showed clearly before they hatched on the fifteenth
day after they were laid.

The caterpillars were one eighth of an inch long,
with black, round, shining heads.   Their bodies were
deep yellow, almost orange.   The first segment had a
black, polished dorsal plate, the second two long black
horns, bifid at tip and projecting over the head; the
anal segment had one long horn, not as long as those
on the second segment, and three shorter tubercles;
the other segments had six short tubercles, those on
the dorsum being longer than the others.   All the
horns and tubercles were rough with spines.   The legs
were shining black, as was the anal plate.   The props
were yellow, with black dots.

The little caterpillars lived in a colony, but not in
close rows like *io* or *caryæ*.   They ate oak and grew to

Anisota stigma.

be three eighths of an inch long, when they molted for the first time, a week after hatching.

Their heads were shining black, bilobed, with a deep median suture. Their bodies were black, with an orange subdorsal line. The legs and props were black, and the horns and tubercles were as before.

Five days later they molted again. Their heads came out large, oval, and orange-brown. Their bodies were black, with an orange dorsal plate on the first segment. The long dorsal horns were black studded with white spines; the shortest tubercles were white The legs, props, and anal plate were shining black After this they separated, and each lived by itself.

In five days they molted a third time, and were seven eighths of an inch long. Their heads were oval, deep orange-brown, and very smooth. Their bodies were orange, with a black transverse band, thickly set with white spines, on the front of each segment. The whole body was studded with black and white spines. The dorsal horns were all longer than before. The legs were deep ocher-brown, with black tips; the abdominal props ocher, with a black band at base and black and white spines. The anal props and plate were deep orange-brown, with a few black, and more white, spines. The spiracles were black encircled with white.

Six days later they molted for the fourth time, coming out an inch and a quarter long. Their heads were large, ocher-brown, with a deep median suture, and smooth. Their bodies were ocher-brown, striped with black and rough with white dots. Their legs were clear ocher-brown, the props black dotted with white, and the anal plate was ocher-brown dotted with white and edged with six black spines. The spiracles were black encircled with white. The first segment had only raised dots instead of spines. There was a substigmatal ridge which was very noticeable.

Nine days later they grew yellower and stopped eating, having grown to a length of about two and a half inches. They go into the earth out of doors, but in the house they stiffened, turned on their backs, and lay so for four days, when the pupæ cast the larvaskins and appeared bright red-brown, with two bright red, oval tubercles at the back of the thorax. They turned almost black in a day or two, tubercles and all, and measured one and one eighth inches in length. They were rough, with short abdominal spines, and were not polished like sphingid pupæ or those of *A. torrefacta*.

The pupæ work their way to the surface of the earth when the moth is ready to emerge, and we have found the empty pupa-cases part-way out of the ground in the early summer.

The caterpillars are rather common where oaks abound. They are single-brooded, and may be found from June till October, their range extending from Canada to Georgia — possibly farther south — and far West. They are not as common as *A. senatoria*, and are larger and handsomer.

Their long horns are movable, but seem of no use as protective resemblance or bird-frighteners.

There is one record of their spines' stinging, but we have handled the caterpillars repeatedly without the least urtication, and as only one man records such stinging experience we feel that there must have been some mistake.

The larvæ are to be found on low-growing oaks, their anal props fixed on a twig or leaf-stem, and their bodies lying along the edge of the leaf on which they are, or have been, feeding, for they frequently rest where they have fed, their horns standing out like the points of an oak-leaf, although they cannot be said to resemble the leaf.

The moths are not very pretty. They are ocher-brown, more or less suffused with pinkish purple. The fore wings are crossed by a purplish line, and are thickly dotted with black. There is a conspicuous white discal dot. The hind wings are less dotted, more purplish, and crossed by a purplish band. The male is smaller than the female, but has similar marks, and his antennæ are broadly pectinate at the basal half and simple at the tip. The female's antennæ are simple throughout their length. Like all the ceratocampids, *stigma* has a small head, a large thorax and abdomen, and is very "furry" in parts.

The larvæ are said to live on hazel and chestnut as well as oak, but we have found them on oak only, and more on red and scrub oaks than on any other.

DRYOCAMPA RUBICUNDA

GENUS, DRYOCAM'PA (forest caterpillar).
SPECIES, RUBICUN'DA ("rosy").

"These bugs are eating up a lady's maple-tree. It 's
a cut-leaved maple, and she does n't want it killed, so
she sent me to have the Bug-woman tell me what to do
about it."

One of Us was "the Bug-woman" to the farm-folk
about a small village, and the messenger was a man
who cut grass, hoed potatoes, and weeded flower-beds
for the ladies of the place.

The message was a very common one, and we had
often been called from the dinner-table by a summons
to go and take "some awful big worms," or "terrible
big bugs," off the trees and shrubs in the village, while
men and women with tomato-cans of crawlers frequently appeared in the evening, after the farm-work
was done, for us to name and tell "all about" them,
that meaning all about the possible harm to crops or
trees, and the danger of being stung, bitten, or poisoned
by them; for in the country there is a firm belief in the
poisonous qualities of all crawling things, and tremen-
dous tales are told, and fully believed, of the results of
"poisonous" caterpillar bites.

Therefore the message did not surprise us at all, and

286

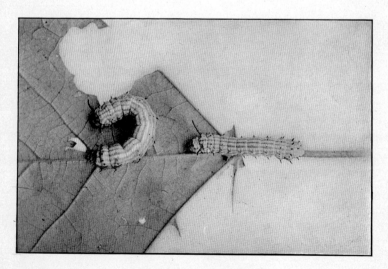

Dryocampa rubicunda.

we opened the box. In it were seven beautiful caterpillars, light green, striped lengthwise with dark green, and having one rose-red stripe on each side, and two long black horns projecting over the head.

"Is it a large tree?" asked One of Us.

"No, ma'am; it 's only been set out a couple of years."

"Then the best thing to do is to pick off all the caterpillars and bring them to me. I will pay for them."

"There ain't no caterpillars there. It 's only these bugs."

"These are caterpillars, not bugs."

"Oh, no; caterpillars 've got fur all over them. Some folks call these worms and some calls 'em bugs. I call 'em bugs."

"Yes, I know you did, but that does not make them so. They are caterpillars whether they have hairs or not. There are probably not enough to do any serious harm now, but there will be a second brood unless these are all picked off, so you had better pick all you can and bring them to me. I will take care of them and pay you for them."

The crawlers were nearly full fed and soon stopped eating. Out of doors they go into the ground to pupate, but these crawled about the tins for a time and then lay quiet and pupated finely.

In about twelve days a pretty little moth emerged, pale yellow and pink, and very lively. Its simple antennæ showed it to be female, and she began laying eggs before dark. Of course these eggs were of no use — sixty unfertilized eggs. Such a waste!

The next day two males emerged, and evidently one of them mated with the female, for all the eggs she laid after that, ninety in two nights, hatched in due season.

The eggs were small, very round-oval, clear golden yellow, but grew orange, then brown, then greenish gray. Then the shells became perfectly transparent, showing the brown heads and yellowish bodies of the larvæ curled up in the eggs.

They hatched on the eighteenth day, another lot hatching thirteen days, after they were laid.

The little caterpillars were about an eighth of an inch long, with shining black heads and yellow bodies. There were two black dorsal lines, and on the second segment were two yellow tubercles, each ending in two setæ. There were sparse short setæ on the body. The legs were almost black, the props yellow. They grew greener with food, but would eat only soft maple and cut-leaved maple. From sugar-maple they crawled away with every appearance of dislike. They fed and lived in close rows on leaves. Two days later they were light green striped length-wise with dark green, the dorsal line being darkest.

On the seventh day they molted, the other brood molting on the tenth day. Their heads were polished black, their bodies green striped with darker green, and having on the first segment four raised dots of shining black; on the second two long black dorsal horns; on the eleventh a transverse row of short, sharp, black spines; on the anal shield a V-shaped tubercle, and two spines like those on the eleventh segment; the other segments had six short, sharp, shining black spines on each. The legs were shining black, the props green with a black spot on each.

On the twelfth day after hatching they molted again. This time the first segment had a shining black dorsal plate, and the anal shield was edged with sharp black spines; the tenth and eleventh segments were spread out wider than any of the others at the substigmatal edge. Otherwise they were not changed. A few had umber-brown heads.

On the twenty-first day after hatching they molted for the third time. Their heads were all umber-brown, and their bodies were striped black and yellow, the venter being black. Their legs and abdominal props were black, the anal props black and yellow. The long horns on the second segment became filaments; the other spines were as before. The caterpillars varied, some being distinctly black and yellow, others black and pale green, others dark green and light green. The black plate on the first segment was a single transverse plate in some, two patches in others, four dots in others. In some the venter was black, in others dark green, in others pale olive-green. Some had a pinkish stripe on the substigmatal line of the tenth and eleventh segments; others had not.

They fed for eleven days, and then surprised us by not molting again, but lying quiet for pupation. They were about two inches long. Five days later the pupæ appeared. From egg to pupa was thirty-seven days, ending late in September.

The caterpillars lived near each other, "socially," through all their larval life, but were not close together in rows after the second molt. We have often found

19

them on the maple-trees, two or three on a leaf, and fifteen or twenty on the five or six leaves nearest the first we found.

They are very pretty caterpillars, and are very dainty, refusing leaves not absolutely fresh, and by no means willing to eat any kind of maple which may be most convenient. We had to walk a mile and a quarter to get leaves which suited this brood, and to go as often as every second day, too, and then they refused the leaves from the older tree, and would eat only those from saplings, which do not keep fresh as long as tree-leaves, even after soaking their twigs.

The pupæ were small, dull black, rough with spines on the edges of the abdominal segments.

The moths are beautiful. They have pale yellow bodies and pink, "furry" legs. The fore wings are pink at the base and apex, with a triangular patch of pale yellow between the two pink areas. The hind wings are yellow at base, shading into pink. The yellow is the pale yellow of primroses. The male's antennæ are pectinate on the lower half, simple the rest of their length. The female's are simple.

Leucarctia acræa.

Leucarctia acræa.

XIV

ARCTIIDÆ

FAMILY, ARCTI'IDÆ
SUBFAMILY, ARCTII'NÆ.

LEUCARCTIA ACRÆA

GENUS, LEUCARC'TIA ("white bear": the ♀ moth is white).
SPECIES, ACRÆ'A.

THESE are the fox-colored "woolly bears" which hurry across the walks and roads in the autumn; the "old-fashioned caterpillars" they are called by some of our friends who used to call all smooth caterpillars "worms." Sometimes they are yellow, instead of fox-colored, or cream-colored, or even really white, but they "make the same moth in the end." We tried, one year, rearing all the differently colored ones in boxes, each color in its separate box, then kept the cocoons separate, and in the following spring we had a fine lot of *acræa* moths. The male has orange hind wings, and all have orange abdomens with black spots. The black speckles on the wings vary much in number.

HALESIDOTA TESSELLATA

GENUS,　HALESIDO'TA.
SPECIES,　TESSELLA'TA　("tessellated," "checked").

These very common little crawlers may be silver-gray, brownish gray, "old gold," or even a brighter yellow. They are shaped like *H. caryæ*, but have no "black buttons down the back," though they have long pencils like those of *caryæ*.

They eat almost any leaf and are very active. They spin close, compact cocoons, much like those of *caryæ*.

The moth is similar to *caryæ* also, but paler, and has the patagia edged with pale peacock-blue.

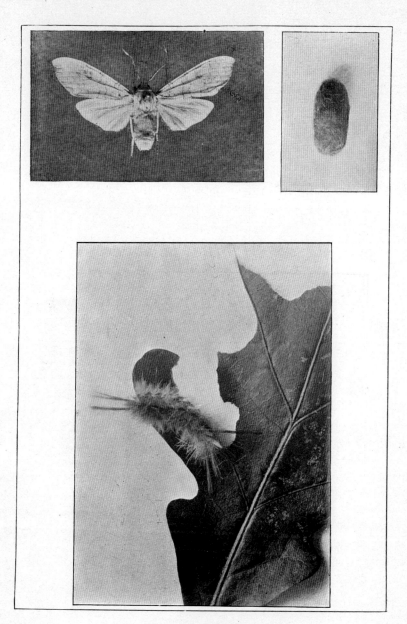

Halesidota tessellata.

a.

Euclea cippus and Isa inornata.

XV

LIMACODIDÆ

FAMILY, LIMACO'DIDÆ.

EUCLEA CIPPUS

GENUS, EUCLE'A.
SPECIES, CIP'PUS (*a* in the picture).

THIS is a limacodid caterpillar, very pretty, green, with yellow and red marks. It is found on maple, plum, pear, willow, wild cherry, and this one was on a solitary sweetbrier far from any tree or other shrub. It ate maple, however. It spins a cocoon. The moth is a pretty little one, reddish brown, with some green marks on the fore wings. The species is common..

ISA INORNATA

GENUS,   I'SA.

SPECIES,   INORNA'TA.

This limacodid larva is found on maple and bayberry, and probably on other plants. It is very pretty from the fringe of spinose tubercles around the edge of the body. It is green in color. It makes a pretty little moth, not very common. It spins a cocoon.

Datana major.

Datana major.

XVI

NOTODONTIDÆ

FAMILY, NOTODON'TIDÆ.

DATANA MAJOR

GENUS, DATA'NA.
SPECIES, MA'JOR ("larger").

BARE stems of *Andromeda ligustrina* and bunches of yellow, or white, and black just below the bare stems show two habits of *Datana major* caterpillars. They live in very close crowds until almost full fed, and they begin at the top leaf of a branch and eat downward.

The photograph shows their position at rest, but does not show that their heads are red, or that their bodies are yellow, or white, and black in stripes.

They have an unpleasant habit of ejecting partly digested food when disturbed. They are locally very abundant, but also much victimized by parasitic flies.

The moths are brown, with lines of darker brown.

CERATOCAMPIDÆ

FAMILY, CERATOCAM'PIDÆ.

ANISOTA SENATORIA

GENUS, ANISO'TA.
SPECIES, SENATO'RIA.

These caterpillars are often found in colonies on oaks, and sometimes in numbers enough to defoliate the trees. In some places they are very destructive.

They are black and yellow or orange in longitudinal stripes, and have spines and "horns" like those of *A. stigma.* Their spines are said to sting like nettles if they pierce the skin, but we have never had any trouble of the kind in handling them. They pupate in the ground.

In the South they are double-brooded. The moths are ocher-brown, speckled with black, and having a white discal dot on each fore wing.

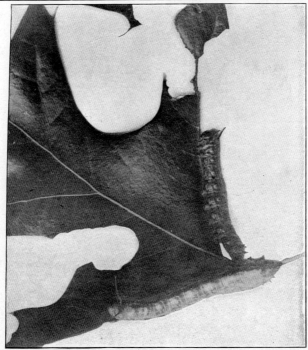

Anisota senatoria.

Acronycta americana.

XVII

NOCTUINA

FAMILY,   NOCTUI'NA.
SUBFAMILY,   NOCTU'IDÆ.

ACRONYCTA AMERICANA

GENUS,   ACRONYC'TA.
SPECIES,   AMERICA'NA.

THIS is the cream-white or pale straw-colored caterpillar common on maple. It is reported on other
trees also, but we have never succeeded in making it
eat anything but maple. It is a very slow caterpillar
both in motion and in growth, and is almost the same in
appearance from the earliest stage to the latest,— that
is, from egg to cocoon,— except in size. Sometimes
the larvæ grow very large, measuring over two inches
in length. They spin cocoons.

The moths are white and gray, with black dots and
dashes.

ACRONYCTA HASTULIFERA

GENUS, ACRONYC'TA.
SPECIES, HASTULIF'ERA ("spear bearing": from marks like spear-heads on
the wings).

We have found hundreds of these caterpillars on alder, and some on willow. They vary in color from pale chocolate-brown to deep chocolate, and are sometimes of a pale yellow-brown, always dark between the segments, and have dark pencils on the dorsum. When disturbed they curl up and drop from the plant, like the " woolly bears."

They are subject to fungoid diseases which kill many of them, and their stiff bodies may be found on branches of the alders, apparently unharmed, but they break at a touch and are filled with fungoid growth. Parasites kill many of them also. They spin cocoons.

Acronycta hastulifera.

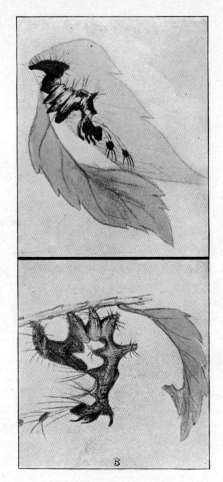

Harrisimemna trisignata.

HARRISIMEMNA TRISIGNATA

GENUS, HARRISIMEM'NA.
SPECIES, TRISIGNA'TA ("thrice-marked").

The first sight of this queer caterpillar is usually mis-
leading, for the cast masks which adhere to the long
hairs over the head are of a dirty orange-color, and
look like drops of decayed animal matter, while the
black, white, and dirty yellow of the caterpillar and
its shaking and waggling from side to side make it
look like a mass of unpleasantness, and it needs a
second look to show that it is alive. It may be found
on spiræa, lilac, and other shrubs. When disturbed it
hangs as in B, and gives its body a most peculiar motion, utterly unlike any other living thing we have ever
seen. Gibson gives an excellent description of it in
one of his books or magazine articles.

The sketches given here were taken from the first
caterpillar we found, just before it bored into a bit of
rotten wood to pupate.

INDEX

It is usual to add to the name of an insect the abbreviated name of the entomologist who named the species.